REPORT

Second-Language Skills for All?

Analyzing a Proposed Language Requirement
for U.S. Air Force Officers

Chaitra M. Hardison • Louis W. Miller • Jennifer J. Li • Amber N. Schroeder •
Susan Burkhauser • Sean Robson • Deborah Lai

Prepared for the United States Air Force

PROJECT AIR FORCE

The research described in this report was sponsored by the United States Air Force under Contract FA7014-06-C-0001. Further information may be obtained from the Strategic Planning Division, Directorate of Plans, Hq USAF.

Library of Congress Cataloging-in-Publication Data

Second language skills for all? : analyzing a proposed language requirement for U.S. Air Force officers / Chaitra M. Hardison ... [et al.].
    p. cm.
  Includes bibliographical references.
  ISBN 978-0-8330-6034-1 (pbk. : alk. paper)
  1. United States. Air Force—Officers—Training of. 2. Second language acquisition—United States. 3. Communicative competence—United States. I. Hardison, Chaitra M.

  UG638.S43 2012
  358.4'161—dc23

                                                                                    2012041174

The RAND Corporation is a nonprofit institution that helps improve policy and decisionmaking through research and analysis. RAND's publications do not necessarily reflect the opinions of its research clients and sponsors.

RAND® is a registered trademark.

Published 2012 by the RAND Corporation
1776 Main Street, P.O. Box 2138, Santa Monica, CA 90407-2138
1200 South Hayes Street, Arlington, VA 22202-5050
4570 Fifth Avenue, Suite 600, Pittsburgh, PA 15213-2665
RAND URL: http://www.rand.org/
To order RAND documents or to obtain additional information, contact
Distribution Services: Telephone: (310) 451-7002;
Fax: (310) 451-6915; Email: order@rand.org

Preface

Many federal entities, including Congress, the Department of Defense, and the military services, are concerned about the language capabilities of the armed forces. This report documents the results of a study of Air Force officers that was conducted in response to a suggestion from the Foreign Policy Advisor to the Chief of Staff of the Air Force that the Air Force should require all Air Force officers to achieve a specific, high level of proficiency in a language other than English as a prerequisite for commissioning. Our research addressed the following two broad questions: First, would it be feasible to require all new Air Force officers to demonstrate a high degree of proficiency in a second language upon commissioning? Second, what are the potential consequences of implementing a language proficiency requirement for officers?

The research reported here was sponsored by the Foreign Policy Advisor to the Chief of Staff of the Air Force and conducted within the Manpower, Personnel, and Training Program of RAND Project AIR FORCE as part of a fiscal year 2009–2010 study, "Developing Officer Language Proficiency." This report should be of interest to those involved in language or cross-cultural training, Air Force leadership and staff, the broader defense community, government agencies involved in international assignments, any public or private organizations operating in an international environment, and educators interested in K–12 or adult foreign-language education.

RAND Project AIR FORCE

RAND Project AIR FORCE (PAF), a division of the RAND Corporation, is the U.S. Air Force's federally funded research and development center for studies and analyses. PAF provides the Air Force with independent analyses of policy alternatives affecting the development, employment, combat readiness, and support of current and future air, space, and cyber forces. Research is conducted in four programs: Force Modernization and Employment; Manpower, Personnel, and Training; Resource Management; and Strategy and Doctrine.

Additional information about PAF is available on our website:
http://www.rand.org/paf/

Contents

Figures

Tables

Summary

Many official Department of Defense (DoD) and Air Force sources describe language skills as a key warfighting competency.[1] Given the need to develop the language capabilities of Air Force officers, it has been proposed that all Air Force officers be required to demonstrate a high level of proficiency in a foreign language at the time they are commissioned. The Foreign Policy Advisor to the Air Force Chief of Staff asked Project AIR FORCE to evaluate how best to achieve this goal.

In response, we reviewed relevant background information and research on adult language learning and designed and fielded a survey of Air Force officers to address the following:

1. Is a minimum score of 2/2 (limited working proficiency) or 3/3 (general working proficiency) on a language exam a feasible and achievable goal?[2]
2. What potential consequences would implementing a language proficiency requirement for officers have?

Survey of Air Force Officers

Our survey of Air Force officers yielded important insights into the current status of language skills of recent college graduates, the likely outcomes of various types of college language experiences, and the effects of proposed policies on key Air Force outcomes—all important considerations in establishing a language commissioning policy.

Specifically, we designed survey items that addressed each of the following:

- What language skills do current Air Force officers possess?
- Which types of language learning experiences are associated with the highest levels of language skills?
- Are there positive relationships between language skills and various desirable outcomes?
- How would language learning and mandatory language proficiency policies be perceived by officers?
- What do officers perceive as incentives and disincentives for learning a language?

---

[1] See, for instance, DoD, 2005; U.S. Air Force, 2009; and DoD, 2010.

[2] The proficiency levels here are those described in the federal Interagency Language Roundtable (ILR) Proficiency Guidelines, which rate language proficiency on a scale from 0 to 5; detailed descriptions of these skill levels are available on the website (ILR, 2011c). DoD Instruction 5160.70, 2007, and DoD Directive 5160.41E, 2010, also refer to these guidelines as DoD's official measure for foreign-language proficiency.

The survey sample was designed to be representative of the entire officer population.[3] Our survey invitation reached approximately 11,500 current Air Force officers and yielded 3,519 completed responses. Below, we summarize the key survey findings. We then offer our conclusions, which answer the two overall research questions, and provide five recommendations to inform future Air Force language policies.

The Language Skills of Current Air Force Officers

We examined current officers' language skills: their levels of language skill and in which languages. We found that overall, officers have second-language skills that permit only limited interactions in the language. Most would not meet a 2/2 requirement and would require additional training to do so. Although more than 150 languages were represented, the top three were Spanish, German, and French. Unfortunately, these three languages, while commonly taught in the United States, do not address critical national security language needs. Thus, the skills of the officers who did know a second language were not necessarily aligned with Air Force needs.

The Language-Learning Experiences Associated with Greater Proficiency

We explored whether the following types of experiences were associated with greater proficiency:

- majoring or minoring in foreign studies rather than engineering or any other subject
- learning through formal immersion or at home rather than in a classroom
- learning voluntarily or because of mandatory college requirements
- having completed more versus fewer college language courses.

Those who majored or minored in a language or foreign studies reported substantially greater second-language skills than did those with other majors. However, fewer than 50 percent of them reported skills at 2+ or higher. These findings suggest that, if such individuals did not consistently reach a level 2, it is unrealistic to expect those not majoring or minoring in the language to do so.

Those with immersion experiences tended to have higher proficiencies than those without immersion experiences. However, we could not determine whether the immersion itself led to the higher proficiency or the more proficient sought out immersion experiences. Those who had learned a second language at home were much more proficient than those who had not. These findings suggest that immersion may be an important component of language training for this population. They also confirm that those who learned a second language in the home are more likely to have acquired higher levels of second-language proficiency prior to commissioning.

We found that those who had been required to take language courses reported lower proficiencies than those who had taken the courses voluntarily. This suggests that simply requiring officers to learn a language might not yield proficiencies as high as one that motivates individuals to do so voluntarily.

---

[3] We used a complex stratified random sampling plan with oversampling of key groups to select our survey sample. Responses were statistically weighted to represent the officer population.

We also examined the relationship between the number of semesters of college language courses and self-reported proficiency. Those who had taken five courses or more were much more likely to report proficiencies of 1+ or higher. Therefore, to get officers to a 1+ or higher, the minimum number of recommended college-level language courses would be five.

Relationships Between Language Skills and Other Desirable Outcomes

In proposing an officer-corps–wide language requirement, Air Force policymakers have considered other beneficial outcomes, such as an increased desire to learn and capability of learning new languages and increased interest in and tolerance of other cultures.

In our survey, those with higher language proficiency expressed greater interest in and tolerance for other cultures. This could mean that learning a language changes one's attitudes toward other cultures, but it could mean that those more tolerant of and interested in other cultures are more likely to learn a language and be successful at it.

Similarly, those with higher second-language proficiencies were more likely to be interested in learning another language in the near future. In contrast, those with no second-language experience tended not to express such an interest.

These findings suggest that a language requirement could help bring about some of the other outcomes Air Force policymakers have associated with the language requirement.

Views of Officers on a Mandatory Second-Language Proficiency Policy

While an overwhelming majority of officers agreed that language proficiency is important for mission success, far fewer viewed it as relevant to individual career success. This finding suggests a lack of alignment between organizational priorities and individual career priorities. Any mandatory language policy would need to address this important issue. The responses were about evenly divided on the question of whether all officers should be required to know a second language.

Conclusions

Is It Feasible for All Officers to Have Working Proficiency in a Second Language?

The short answer for the near term is *no*. Fewer officer applicants would be eligible for commissioning if a mandatory officer-wide language requirement were in place. Very few officer applicants would meet a 2/2 or 3/3 proficiency level simply by taking a few college language courses or even through heritage language learning or study abroad.[4] It would take a minimum of five semesters of language study in college to reach the 2/2 level in an easy (category I) language, such as Spanish, French, or Italian.

---

[4] For this report, *heritage speakers* refers to those who acquired their second language through exposure to family and/or ties to ethnic communities, whether in the United States or not. This includes immigrants, those with immediate family members who had immigrated, and those whose family immigrated in previous generations but continued to use the heritage language. The research literature has no single definition of this term (Kagan and Dillon, 2008; Montrul, 2009), but ours is consistent with Valdes (2000), whose widely cited definition is an "individual raised in a home where a non-English language is spoken, who speaks or merely understands the heritage language, and who is to some degree bilingual in English and the heritage language."

Training officers who do not already meet the requirement would be resource-intensive and burdensome, requiring at least 26 weeks of intensive study to reach 2/2 in a category I (easy) language (such as Spanish, French, and Italian) and 64 weeks for a category IV (difficult) language (such as Modern Standard Arabic, Mandarin Chinese, Korean, and Pashto), which includes languages of strategic importance. And because of differences among learners, even this intensive language training could not guarantee a 2/2 outcome.

What Are the Potential Consequences of a Language Commissioning Requirement for All Officers?

A policy like the one under discussion could change characteristics of the officer force in many ways, some positive and some negative. The requirement would raise the language skills of officers. However, the types of languages spoken, the extent to which they are maintained, and the extent to which the Air Force utilizes the resulting skills are all major factors in determining how beneficial this would be on a practical level.

The pool of individuals eligible for commissioning would certainly be smaller, and this could affect several other aspects of the officer force. For example, the personality, technical background, and demographic makeup of commissioned officers could change.[5]

The policy would risk dissatisfaction among candidates and current officers, which could reduce organizational commitment and increase turnover. Tying language proficiency to other career milestones could motivate those who already possess language skills and could deter some from joining the Air Force who do not possess the skills and would be forced to acquire them.

Finally, the tendency for language proficiency to diminish without maintenance means the Air Force would need to devote resources to maintaining the skills of those who do not regularly use their language skills in their jobs or social networks.

Recommendations

From the literature review and the conclusions we drew from our survey, we developed key recommendations for Air Force language policy. The subsections below describe each and offer potential consequences.

Tailor Policies to Desired Outcomes, Including Different Policies for Different Outcomes

There are at least five distinctly different desired outcomes of Air Force language policies:

- development and maintenance of language professionals
- having a variety of officers in all types of jobs who can speak to and understand host nationals in their native languages
- having a variety of personnel in all types of jobs that can interact with host nationals in a culturally competent manner

---

[5] Selecting only people who are proficient at a 2/2 or higher could yield a more homogeneous group of officers with respect to personality. Given that personality is related to other workplace outcomes, including unrelated aspects of job performance, the relationships between language proficiency and personality need to be better understood to forestall unintended detrimental effects on other important workplace outcomes. See Chapter Two for more information on language proficiency and personality.

- making all personnel more culturally sensitive and aware
- having a force of personnel able to learn other languages more easily and quickly than otherwise.

These outcomes differ from one another in the policies likely to be required for success. Teasing apart the various outcomes in this way will help clarify which ones are best addressed by language commissioning policies and which are better addressed in other ways. Also, any given outcome will most likely require multiple supporting polices. Tailoring each policy to the specific outcome also significantly increases the likelihood of success. Each objective will thus also require distinct lines of funding and oversight.

Make Language Requirements for Commissioning Flexible, and Include a Variety of Incentives and Opportunities

Officer candidates enter college with a wide variety of second-language skill levels and meet different types of language-learning opportunities. Moreover, languages and majors are not all alike. Some languages are easier to learn than others; some majors, such as engineering, have such full courseloads that they cannot readily accommodate language coursework within a four-year degree program.

Language commissioning policies should accommodate these differences by encouraging improvement at all levels and by rewarding those who attempt to study more-challenging languages. Implementing multiple policies that reward different types of language learning achieves this goal. The following are several examples of policies that, when combined, create a well-balanced and flexible set of language commissioning policies:

- offering scholarships for majoring or minoring in a language
- offering commissioning bonuses for varying levels of proficiency
- providing distance learning courses in strategic languages
- paying for some to spend an extra year in college to concentrate on language study
- requiring two college semesters of language for commissioning, then paying tuition for language courses beyond two semesters
- making more immersion programs available to Reserve Officer Training Corps students
- accommodating waivers and exceptions within the policy for certain groups.

This general approach has certain benefits. For example, a menu approach to college language-learning incentives would increase the depth and range of the language skills of new officers overall without undermining the Air Force's other commissioning goals (e.g., commissioning engineering majors).

The approach would, however, require significant oversight to manage and implement the multiple commissioning policies. Moreover, any of the policies would require dedicated funds and staff (e.g., providing scholarships, commissioning bonuses, and distance learning courses).

Implement Policies for Maintaining and Enhancing Language Skills

Language skills deteriorate quickly through lack of use. Any language policy aimed at officers having certain levels of proficiency at commissioning should be backed up by a plan for maintaining and developing that proficiency after commissioning.

xviii   Second-Language Skills for All? Analyzing a Proposed Language Requirement for U.S. Air Force Officers

Here, too, we recommend an approach that includes multiple types and levels of incentives for improvement and that includes making the time and opportunities for training available. The following are preliminary suggestions:

- Link skill development to career outcomes. Currently, if learning a second language takes time away from an individual's primary duties, it can hinder promotion outcomes.
- Offer increased pay for a variety of language proficiency levels. Add a series of lower-level bonuses for lower-level skills to those already in place for high-level skills.
- Offer a bonus for participation in a structured language-training program. Demonstrating incremental improvement at predetermined points in the training program would earn the bonuses.
- Provide language training during work hours or at times that can accommodate spouse participation.
- Offer temporary duty assignments that utilize language skills, and ensure that they count positively toward promotions.
- Improve records Air Force personnel data systems keep of current and past language proficiency, and use them to make job assignments.

The potential benefits of these policies would include promoting career-long development of language skills and, in turn, enhance the success of language commissioning policies. However, if precommissioning efforts are not linked with such development efforts, language commissioning policies may not yield long-lasting improvements in officer proficiency.

Commissioning policies and career-long development policies are overseen by different Air Force agencies; cooperation among these agencies is vital for the success of this recommendation.

Ensure Buy-In from Air Force Officers at All Levels

Individuals' beliefs about how important a skill is for their careers can affect whether they view developing that skill as worthwhile. While officers tend to view language capabilities as important to the warfighting mission, they believe such skills are less relevant to their own jobs and careers. To change this view, such skills should be tied directly to important career outcomes, including promotions.

Communicating the importance of language skills through words and actions will help institutionalize the role of language proficiency and stress just how important these skills are to the Air Force. Some possible strong signals include

- establishing clear rewards for success
- tying language proficiency to performance evaluations and career outcomes
- making language training programs widely available
- providing time to attend development courses
- making immersion programs available during the regular workday
- offering incentives and extra pay for continuous skill development (even at initially low levels).

A clear and consistent message will require coordination, cooperation, and buy-in from many levels of Air Force leadership. However, only minimal resources would be required beyond those discussed in earlier recommendations.

Evaluate the Success of Each New Program, and Adjust the Program Accordingly

More research is needed on the best ways to implement various language programs and whether they are successful. The most informative efforts will be those that (1) occur after concerted attempts are made to begin implementing new language programs and (2) involve a continuous and systematic process of evaluating programs and informing changes to them. Specifically, the research should involve

- clearly specifying program objectives
- developing and implementing new programs to meet the objectives
- evaluating how well the programs meet the objectives
- researching any other important aspects of the programs
- institutionalizing career-long assessments to identify new training and education needs
- modifying policies based on the new research.

This process is the cornerstone of any well-designed performance improvement intervention and should drive the development of all future Air Force language policies.

Such research efforts would serve to clarify the goals and quantify the success of each program. That information, in turn, would lead to modification or termination of unsuccessful programs. These efforts would also allow continuous assessment of training needs and gaps and could be used to drive policy changes.

These efforts could also help save resources by concentrating them on programs with proven track records, experimental programs aimed at improving success, and new programs intended to fill training gaps.

Execution

To execute these recommendations, we suggest the following:

- Produce a detailed policy statement clearly defining all the intended outcomes for language policies, taking care to distinguish between developing language professionals and developing a language-enabled officer force.
- Offer several precommissioning language opportunities. For each, produce an official statement specifying which specific goal(s) or outcome(s) (from those outlined in the policy statement) the opportunity is aimed at achieving.
- Offer postcommissioning programs aimed directly at continuing and improving language proficiency acquired in response to the precommissioning policies. For each, produce an official statement specifying which specific goal(s) or outcome(s) (from those outlined in the policy statement) the opportunity is aimed at achieving.
- Implement new policies that tie language proficiency to career success and institute a campaign directed toward all levels of the Air Force to gain their buy-in on the importance of language proficiency for every Air Force job.

- Examine the effectiveness of each new precommissioning and postcommissioning program at achieving its stated goals, and evaluate the success of efforts to gain buy-in. Adjust programs and policies using the results of that research.

Given the clear consensus that language skills are important, there is little argument that a language-proficient officer force is a worthwhile aim for the Air Force. Our research points to the most effective, efficient, and realistic means for achieving that vision and shows that there are important trade-offs that would occur in striving to meet it that must be considered.

Acknowledgments

We are especially indebted to our sponsor, Donald M. Bishop, Foreign Policy Advisor to the Chief of Staff of the Air Force. It was his vision for strengthening foreign-language proficiency among Air Force officers that was the motivation for this project. We appreciate the encouragement and many ideas received from Col Jeff Shivnen, Col Dave Simon, Col Tracy Szczepaniak, and Lt Col Jennifer Parenti, all of whom served in the policy advisor's office while our research was in progress, and offer special thanks to Lt Col John Yocum for expediting the final signoff on our report. Col Daniel Uribe, head of the language department at the United States Air Force Academy (USAFA), familiarized us with the language program at USAFA and shared the results of his own research. Also at USAFA, we appreciate time spent with us and valuable insights from Brig Gen Dana Born, Dean of the Faculty, and Brig Gen (Ret) Gunther Mueller. Johnny Weissmuller at the Air Force Personnel Center provided us with information on language testing within the Air Force. At Maxwell AFB, Lt Col Brian Smith introduced us to the Language Enabled Airman Program (LEAP) along with noteworthy ideas. Also at Maxwell, Col John McCain, AETC AFROTC/CC, welcomed us and arranged a series of briefings on how AFROTC is engaged with language instruction.

This research also would not have been possible without the efforts of several RAND researchers. Al Robbert provided invaluable feedback on earlier drafts of this report. Judy Mele at RAND supported the project with abstracts of Air Force data that were crucial for drawing the sample and to supplement information on the survey. Paul Howe provided valuable assistance by gathering needed literature as well as providing information about and insight into Air Force policies and language instruction at the Defense Language Institute Foreign Language Center. Herb Shukiar and several students from the Pardee RAND Graduate School tested out the online survey and provided detailed feedback. Albert Weerman, Bart Orriens, and Tania Gutsche assisted with RAND's Multimode Interviewing Capability (MMIC) tool. Bart Orriens took on the huge job of programming the survey and was gracious and responsive in coping with the complexity of the survey and our frequent requests for changes.

We also are grateful for the efforts of our internal and external reviewers, Sarah Meadows and William Rivers, whose thoughtful comments resulted in numerous improvements to the final report.

Most of all, we thank the more than 3,500 Air Force officers who took the time and effort to respond to our survey.

Abbreviations

ACTFL	American Council on the Teaching of Foreign Languages
AF	Air Force
AFPAK	Afghanistan-Pakistan
CYOS	commissioned years of service
DLAB	Defense Language Aptitude Battery
DLI	Defense Language Institute
DLIFLC	Defense Language Institute Foreign Language Center
DLPT	Defense Language Proficiency Test
DoD	Department of Defense
FLMM	foreign-language or foreign-area studies major or minor
ILR	Interagency Language Roundtable
NSEP	National Security Education Program
PAF	Project AIR FORCE
ROTC	Reserve Officer Training Corps
TDY	temporary duty
USAFA	U.S. Air Force Academy

CHAPTER ONE

Introduction

Despite being home to many different nationalities, ethnicities, and cultures, the United States lags far behind most other countries in second-language proficiency. For example, 56 percent of Europeans can hold a conversation in at least two languages; 28 percent can do so in at least three; and nearly all students are required to study a second language in elementary school (European Commission, 2007). In contrast, only 17 percent of the U.S. population is bilingual (Grosjean, 2010), and only 15 percent of public elementary schools even offer foreign-language education (Rhodes and Pufahl, 2009). This shortfall in second-language education has serious implications for U.S. national security, diplomacy, and overall global competitiveness: The U.S. Air Force, the Department of Defense (DoD), and many other U.S. organizations face a deficit of second-language skills within the adult workforce.

Increasing the Language Proficiency of Incoming Air Force Officers

A number of official DoD documents stress that increasing language skills is vital to national security.[1]

U.S. Air Force (2009) acknowledges that language policy should go beyond the needs of language-intensive jobs and lays out a plan of action for developing the Air Force's foreign cultural, regional, and language skills. It discusses two categories of airmen requiring second-language skills: the foreign-language professional, described as "career language professionals with demonstrated, sustained language skills," and the foreign-language enabled, characterized as "total force Airmen with appropriate and timely language ability to meet tactical mission requirements."[2]

Although both categories are vital for meeting the Air Force's second-language proficiency needs, this report focuses on building capability in the one for which policy is still neither well defined nor well studied: the foreign-language enabled.[3]

---

[1] These include the *Quadrennial Defense Review* (DoD, 2010); DoD, 2005; DoD, 2007a; DoD Instruction 5160.70, 2007; DoD Directive 3000.05, 2005; DoD, 2007b.

[2] Presumably, the foreign-language professional category would include such officer career fields as the regional affairs and political affairs specialists and such enlisted career fields as cryptologic linguist.

[3] For foreign-language professional career fields, the Defense Language Institute (DLI) has well-established methods for identifying personnel with greater language-learning potential and providing intensive language instruction tailored to career-specific needs. No such methods exist for identifying or developing the language enabled.

In 2009, Donald M. Bishop, the Foreign Policy Advisor to the Chief of Staff at that time, proposed requiring all Air Force officers to be proficient in a second language and asked RAND Project AIR FORCE to examine how best to implement this policy.

RAND's Study

The specific proposal was that, by 2016, the Air Force would require all officer candidates to meet a minimum level of proficiency in a second language at the time of commissioning. The proposed level was a score of "3" or "2+" on the Defense Language Proficiency Test (DLPT), which is fairly high proficiency.[4]

A number of rationales would support such an aggressive language commissioning policy. One is that it would send a clear message to current and prospective Air Force officers, the U.S. public, and the international community that the Air Force not only values language proficiency but also demands it as a core competency. A second is that it might, over time, encourage future Air Force hopefuls to pursue language proficiency at earlier ages and encourage their peers to join them. If successful, it could ultimately affect how the other services, other DoD agencies, and even U.S. society view second-language education. Third, the policy advisor's staff and other Air Force personnel anticipated that such a policy could have a number of other beneficial outcomes, such as greater awareness and tolerance of other cultures, increased ease and speed of learning additional languages on just-in-time and as-needed bases, and increased ability of Air Force leaders to compete for senior joint and theater command assignments. These changes in the qualities of Air Force officers served as motivation for the proposal.

At the same time, the degree to which such an ambitious policy could be successful was unclear, given how little second-language instruction most U.S. college graduates receive. Therefore, having been asked to examine and recommend approaches to developing language proficiency in officer accession programs, we instead suggested exploring more-fundamental questions about the feasibility and consequences of such a policy.

The literature on best practices for teaching foreign languages is extensive and can inform curriculum development. It is not possible, however, to relate specific educational experiences—both kind and amount—to specific levels of achievement, especially given the differences among language learners and how the differences affect outcomes. The proposed officer accession language policy would also affect a very specific and unstudied group of individuals (i.e., Air Force officers). We therefore needed to collect data to answer not only the initial research questions but also two additional primary research questions we identified:

1. Is a minimum DLPT score of 2/2 or 3/3 feasible and achievable?
2. What are the potential consequences of implementing a language proficiency requirement for officers?

We took a multifaceted approach to answering these questions. First, we extensively reviewed the literature on second-language acquisition and explored existing Air Force per-

---

[4] This test measures reading, listening, and speaking. Chapter Two describes the scoring system in more detail, but a score reported as "2/2" equates to a reading level of 2 and a listening level of 2. Appendix A describes the skills corresponding to various score levels. Scores of 2+ or 3 represent advanced levels of proficiency and are not likely to be achieved by taking a few courses in college.

sonnel data. Then, we conducted a large-scale, in-depth survey of Air Force officers. This use of a survey produced valuable information about the potential consequences of the proposed officer accession language policy and allowed us to explore these questions via a sample of recently commissioned officers (as proxies for those currently applying for commissions) and in a sample representative of officers in general.

Specifically, our survey elicited officers' experiences with languages, informally assessed their language skills, and asked about their attitudes toward potential language policies. We also elicited officers' views on the rewards, incentives, and obstacles of language learning and of the relevance of second-language skills to the Air Force and to each of them as individuals.

Organization of the Report

Chapter Two presents some relevant background information on adult language learning and draws inferences for an Air Force officer accession language policy. Chapter Three provides an overview of our survey participants and the questions we asked and why. Chapter Four presents detailed analyses of the survey results, and Chapter Five reports our conclusions and recommendations. Six appendixes provide supplemental information: Appendix A presents the Interagency Language Roundtable's (ILR's) language proficiency scale and descriptions of each level of proficiency; Appendix B lists the self-report language assessment we adapted from existing ILR self-assessments for use in our survey; Appendix C lists the existing language flagship programs at colleges and universities across the United States; Appendix D provides screenshots of the main portions of the survey; Appendix E summarizes the number and types of language courses offered in a sample of 50 colleges and universities that host Reserve Officer Training Corps (ROTC) detachments; and Appendix F offers extended details on survey write-in comments.

CHAPTER TWO

Background on Adult Language Learning

This chapter provides background information on selected aspects of language learning that might inform Air Force language policies. It begins with existing definitions of language proficiency, the measurement of language skills, and the classification of languages according to difficulty. It then describes the sources of expertise in languages other than English in the United States. To highlight the effects of variations among adult language learners, we explore some of the individual characteristics known to influence individual outcomes in language learning. Insights into the importance of maintaining language skills once acquired follow. Then, to illustrate the investment of resources required to acquire higher levels of language proficiency, we describe adult language education programs designed to build skills that can be used in a work environment and for government or national security purposes. For each topic, we discuss how the information relates to the proposed officer accession language policy for the Air Force.

Measuring Language Proficiency

We defined language proficiency as "the ability to use language as a tool to get things done" (Jackson and Kaplan, 2003).[1] Among the numerous metrics for measuring language proficiency, the most common scales are the ILR and American Council on the Teaching of Foreign Languages (ACTFL) scales. The ILR scale was initially developed for use in government service in the late 1950s (ILR, 2011b) and has since been revised and refined.[2] The ACTFL scale, developed in the 1980s, is a slightly modified version of the ILR scale and is widely used by the broader language assessment community (ACTFL, 2010).

Both measures use separate scales to describe proficiency in aspects of performance: listening, reading, speaking, and writing proficiency.[3] As an example, Table 2.1 lists each level on the ILR scale for speaking proficiency and a description of the skills associated with each level.

---

[1] We use the terms *language* and *second language* throughout the report to generally refer to languages other than English. Where possible, we use these terms instead of the term *foreign language* to account for the fact that the United States has no official language and that languages other than English are not necessarily foreign to all Americans or to America. The military and other U.S. communities do commonly use the term *foreign* to describe languages other than English. For this reason, we do occasionally use the term *foreign language* in this manuscript when additional clarification is needed (e.g., to distinguish foreign-language majors from English majors) or to be consistent with the terms adopted by the military or other published sources. These general usage rules apply to similar terms in this report, such as *foreign area studies*.

[2] See the ILR website for detailed descriptions of the levels for speaking, reading, writing, and listening used in this scale.

[3] ILR also has scales for translation performance, interpreting performance, audio translation performance, and competence in intercultural communication. See Appendix A for full descriptions of the ILR proficiency levels for speaking, read-

Table 2.1
Correspondences Between ILR and ACTFL Speaking Proficiency Descriptions

ILR Level	ILR Proficiency Description	ACTFL Level
S-0	No functional proficiency	Novice Low Novice Mid
S-0+	Memorized proficiency	Novice High
S-1	Elementary proficiency sufficient to satisfy minimum courtesy requirements and hold very simple conversations on everyday topics	Intermediate Low Intermediate Mid
S-1+	More than elementary but less than limited working proficiency	Intermediate High
S-2	Limited working proficiency sufficient to satisfy routine social demands and limited work requirements	Advanced Low Advanced Mid
S-2+	More than limited working proficiency, but less than general professional proficiency	Advanced High
S-3	General professional proficiency, able to speak the language with sufficient structural accuracy and vocabulary to participate effectively in most formal and informal conversations on practical, social, and professional topics	Superior
S-3+	More than general professional proficiency, but less than advanced professional proficiency	Superior
S-4	Advanced professional proficiency, able to use the language fluently and accurately on all levels normally pertinent to professional needs	Superior
S-4+	More than advanced professional, but less than functionally native proficiency	Superior
S-5	Functionally native proficiency, equivalent to that of a highly educated native speaker	Superior

SOURCE: ACTFL, 1999; ILR, 2011c.

An individual's level on these scales is determined through performance on paper-and-pencil tests, computer-based tests, and/or oral tests. Although many commercial tests are available, the most well established for government and national security use are the DLPT, from the Defense Language Institute Foreign Language Center (DLIFLC), and the ACTFL Oral Proficiency Interview (OPI) and written tests, from Language Testing International, the ACTFL language testing office. Both the ACTFL tests and the DLPT include written and oral components, and both offer tests in a wide variety of strategic languages. The DLPT, however, measures proficiency against the government's ILR scale and is the official test for assessing language proficiency in the Air Force and the other services and DoD.

DLPT scores for listening, reading, and speaking are reported separately. Each skill receives a separate number, with the results recorded in that order, with slashes between them. For example, someone with a score of 2 in listening, a 2+ in reading, and a 1+ in speaking in Arabic would be reported as being a "2/2+/1+" in Arabic. Note, however, that testing generally reflects operational requirements and that individuals are usually tested only in the skills needed for their jobs.

Categories of Difficulty

The degree of similarity between a target language and the language(s) an individual already knows affects the speed at which the learner is likely to master a new language. DLI catego-

---

ing, and listening. For descriptions of the ACTFL scale levels, see ACTFL, 1999.

rizes languages into levels of difficulty based on the number of weeks of intensive instruction (six hours per day, five days a week) typically required for an adult native speaker of English to reach a given level of proficiency, such as 2/2/2.[4]

DLI classifies languages into four categories of difficulty. Category I is the easiest for native English speakers, category IV the most difficult. Table 2.2 lists the languages in each category and the typical number of weeks of intensive study it takes to achieve 2/2/2 in each, assuming learners entering the course have met the required threshold on the Defense Language Aptitude Battery (DLAB).

This information suggests that few would ever meet the 3/3 threshold based on college courses alone in a relatively easy language and even fewer in a language beyond a category I. Given that many of the strategic languages the services need most are category III or IV, any policy that requires language proficiency must take into account the time it takes to learn these more difficult languages.

The Supply of Language Expertise

In the United States, language skills are generally acquired from ethnic heritage communities, the education system, U.S. government language programs, private language services, and outsourcing to foreign countries (Brecht et al., 2004). The U.S. military could conceivably draw from the first four of these; the last, outsourcing to foreign countries, is undesirable for national security reasons. In practice, speakers of languages other than English come to the military primarily from the first three—heritage communities, the education system, and U.S. government language programs.

However, the proficiency levels coming out of these sectors vary greatly. In the United States, individuals who study a second language usually begin late—high school is a common starting point—and continue only for a few years. According to Brecht et al. (2004), only 9 percent of students reach level 2 in listening and only 35 percent in reading for the more difficult languages that are critical for national security.

Table 2.2
DLI Categories of Language Difficulty and Weeks to Achieve a 2/2/2 (L/R/S)

Language Category	Languages	Weeks to Achieve	
		2/2/2	3/3/3
I	French, Italian, Portuguese, Spanish	26	62
II	German	35	87
III	Hebrew, Hindi, Persian Farsi, Dari, Punjabi, Russian, Serbian/Croatian, Tagalog, Thai, Turkish, Uzbek, Urdu	48	120
IV	Modern Standard Arabic, Arabic Iraqi, Chinese, Japanese, Korean, Levantine, Pashto	64	158

SOURCE: DLIFLC Catalog, 2011–2012.

---

[4]   For the Foreign Service Institute (FSI), the targeted levels of proficiency are ILR level 3 in speaking and reading (FSI, 2011). For DLI, they are ILR level 2 in speaking, listening, and reading.

With such limited outcomes from the current education system, the U.S. government and military services could also rely on the heritage sector, which accounts for approximately 18 percent of the U.S. population (Shin and Bruno, 2003). However, heritage speakers also vary widely in proficiency and may need additional training to achieve high proficiency (see, for example, Bermel and Kagan, 2000; Kagan and Dillon, 2008).[5] The other key source of supply is government and military language training programs. The limited supply of individuals with second-language skills would necessarily affect the outcomes of an Air Force second-language requirement. If it planned to train those who did not know a second language, the Air Force would have to acknowledge the many factors that influence individual outcomes, ranging from the extent of exposure, interaction, and instruction to a variety of individual characteristics, which we discuss in the next section.

Individual Differences Among Language Learners

Language learners vary greatly in their ability to master a second or subsequent language. Individual differences, such as age, aptitude, motivation, prior language-learning experience, learning styles, beliefs, culture, gender, and self-direction, can affect the likelihood of success. Air Force policymakers therefore need to understand the characteristics that can affect success and that a policy requiring a second language would eliminate or disqualify those who do not acquire one, which may affect force demographics. Therefore, this section examines the research on a few factors thought to influence language learning: age, aptitude, motivation, cultural openness, personality, and language-learning disability.

Age

It is widely accepted that children and adults learn language differently and that the age when learning begins is a strong predictor of success in learning a language. While young children acquire their first languages naturally with little or no conscious effort, adults typically exert substantial effort to reach nativelike levels of acquisition. For language learning, younger is better, and older is worse.

The critical period hypothesis states that the development of speech has a biological foundation and that the optimal period for first (and second or subsequent) language acquisition ends around adolescence (Lenneberg, 1964; Lennenberg, 1967).[6] Although other researchers have proposed variations on this hypothesis (see, for example, Shachter, 1996; Oyama, 1978; Hakuta, 2001; and Chiswick and Miller, 2007), the idea that outcomes in language learning tend to decline with age is widely supported by scientific research.

---

5 For this report, we define *heritage speakers* as those who acquired their language skills through exposure to family and/or an ethnic community inside or outside the United States. This includes people who immigrated to the United States, people who have immediate family members who immigrated, and people whose family immigrated in previous generations but who continue to use their heritage language. The literature recognizes that there is no single definition for this term (Kagan and Dillon, 2008; Montrul, 2009), but ours is consistent with Valdes (2000), a widely cited definition of a *heritage speaker* as an "individual raised in a home where a non-English language is spoken, who speaks or merely understands the heritage language, and who is to some degree bilingual in English and the heritage language."

6 The beginnings of the hypothesis appear in Lenneberg, 1964. The term "critical period" appeared for the first time in Lenneberg, 1967.

The critical period hypothesis does not imply that an individual's ability to learn languages disappears but rather that automatic acquisition from mere exposure, the mechanism by which a child learns a first language, declines after adolescence (Lenneberg, 1967; DeKeyser and Larson-Hall, 2005). While children's success at learning a second language depends more on memory, adults' success depends more on analytical skill (DeKeyser, 2000; Harley and Hart, 1997; and DeKeyser and Larson-Hall, 2005).

While the Air Force cannot change the factors that lead many Americans not to learn a second language until adolescence or adulthood, we include this research because it confirms what most people know anecdotally—that it usually takes substantial effort for adults to learn a new language. Even with instruction, success is not guaranteed and depends on numerous individual factors, which the following sections address briefly. Again, these individual factors will have implications for the pool of officer candidates.

Language Aptitude

Although the concept of language aptitude is almost universally accepted, it is still not fully defined. In general, it refers to an individual's ability to learn a second or subsequent language and may predict the time required to attain a certain level of language proficiency. Carroll (1981) characterizes language aptitude as comprising four components: phonetic coding ability (the ability to remember and associate sounds with symbols), rote memory capacity, sensitivity to grammar, and inductive language-learning ability. Since then, many others have attempted to reconceptualize language aptitude in varying terms. Skehan (1989) argues that language aptitude consists of three, not four, components: auditory ability, linguistic ability, and memory capacity. Grigorenko, Sternberg, and Ehrman (2000) suggests that language-learning ability is strongly determined by the ability to cope with novelty and ambiguity, among other things. Dornyei (2006) argues that there is no such thing as language aptitude, but instead, a number of cognitive factors make up a composite measure that can be referred to as the learner's overall capacity to learn another language. In comparison with these past efforts to characterize language aptitude, current DoD-funded research takes a broad view of the notion of language aptitude and includes cognitive, perceptual, personality, motivational, and experience factors to predict success in adult language learning (Linck et al., 2010).

Many tests have been developed to measure language aptitude, including the Modern Language Aptitude Test, the Pimsleur Language Aptitude Battery (PLAB), the Cognitive Ability for Novelty in Acquisition of Language-Foreign (CANAL-F) test, the LLAMA tests, and DLAB (Carroll and Sapon, 1958; Pimsleur, 1966; Peterson and Al-Haik, 1976; Grigorenko, Sternberg, and Ehrman, 2000; Meara, 2005). DLI and the military services use the DLAB to classify personnel into language-intensive career fields, such as cryptolinguist, and to predict success potential for more-difficult languages. As mentioned above, DoD is currently funding the development of a new version of the DLAB that accommodates a wide range of individual factors. Although language aptitude varies among individuals, we cannot yet predict exactly how a policy that selects for higher language aptitude might affect Air Force officer demographics, other than being likely to reduce the pool of officer candidates.

Motivation

Motivation is important in almost any kind of learning. However, Gardner and Lambert (1972) argues that motivation for language learning differs from other kinds of learning motivation because the learning task involves not just acquisition of knowledge and skills, but also "identify[ing] with members of another ethnolinguistic group." The authors suggested that an individual's attitudes toward the culture and native speakers of the target language would influence his or her motivation and subsequent language-learning success (Gardner and Lambert, 1972).

A later model of language learning categorizes motivation into two types: integrative, referring to a positive attitude toward a culture and a desire to participate in it as a member, and instrumental, referring to language acquisition for a specific purpose, such as career or education (Gardner, 1985; Gardner, 1988). While Gardner and others have suggested that students with integrative motivation would be more successful than those with instrumental motivation, numerous counterexamples of this theory exist. For example, integrative motivation is less important when newcomer integration into a culture or setting is virtually impossible; conversely, individuals who are not interested in the cultures of their target languages can achieve very high levels of proficiency (Leaver and Atwell, 2002).

Cognitive theories about how motivation influences learning in general distinguish between intrinsic and extrinsic motivations (Deci and Ryan, 1985). Intrinsic motivation comes from within the individual and is related to the person's identity and sense of well being. Extrinsic motivation comes from outside the individual, such as learning for the sake of rewards. Although in practice, an individual's total motivation is usually both intrinsic and extrinsic, there is clear evidence that an extrinsic motivation alone is unlikely to bring learners to high levels of proficiency (see, for example, Dornyei, 2003; Noels, 2001; Noels et al., 2000).

But other factors also affect the likelihood of success. Motivation alone, however it is categorized, has limited influence on outcomes (Dornyei and Schmidt, 2001). This has a bearing on potential Air Force language policies because it is unlikely that extrinsic incentives alone (such as foreign-language bonus pay) will be sufficient to motivate officers to acquire and maintain proficiency in a second (or subsequent) language.

Acculturation and Cultural Openness

Schumann (1978) argued that the learner's degree of acculturation—the social and psychological integration of the learner with native speakers of the target language—could determine the learner's degree of success in acquiring the language. Examples of social integration variables include social distance between the speaker and the target language group, similarity in culture, attitudes of the learner's language group toward the target language group, and intended length of residence in the target culture. Psychological integration variables include language shock (the anxiety of speaking a new language); culture shock (the anxiety of interacting with a new culture); motivation; and ego permeability (the ability to relax personal linguistic inhibitions to embrace the systems of a new language).

Substantial research since 1978 has led to wide acceptance that successful language acquisition requires acculturation or some degree of cultural openness, even if the learner does not wish to become a part of the target culture. A policy that required Air Force officers to know a second language would thus, to some extent, require them to have at least a minimal degree of cultural openness. This work also confirms that language training is more likely to be effective when combined with cultural training.

At the same time, researchers have found that learning another language is associated with positive changes in attitudes and perceptions toward other cultures (Davidson and Lehman, 2005; Robinson, Rivers, and Brecht, 2006). Thus, language learning is associated with higher degrees of cultural openness, and it stands to reason that an Air Force foreign-language requirement could have the secondary consequence of creating an officer corps with a higher degree of cultural openness.

Personality Traits

Although other factors (sometimes referred to as *affective factors* in the language-learning literature[7]) such as attitudes, motivation, and self-efficacy have been examined extensively in the literature, several studies have explored relationships between well-established personality dimensions (such as the "Big Five": extroversion/introversion, emotional stability, openness to experience, conscientiousness, and agreeableness) and language-learning outcomes. Research has established that scores on certain Big Five dimensions are predictors of other important workplace outcomes, including job performance (see, for example, Barrick and Mount, 1991). It is therefore important to understand the relationships between personality and language proficiency to prevent a 2/2 proficiency requirement from causing unintended and possibly undesirable changes in the personality characteristics of the officer force.

Research on the Big Five and language acquisition is still in its infancy, with extroversion/introversion as the trait that has been examined most frequently. Extroversion and introversion are opposite ends of the same continuum. Extroverts (those low in introversion) tend to be outgoing, have many friends, enjoy talking to strangers, enjoy interacting with large groups of people, etc. Introverts (those low in extroversion) tend to enjoy time alone, have a small number of close friends, and are unlikely to seek out attention in large groups.

Some language-learning researchers have found that the best language learners tended to be introverts. For example, Ehrman (2008) found that, among the highest level of learners (near-native, Level 4 on the Foreign Service Institute scale), introversion was one of the traits most heavily represented. The findings on the importance of introversion in language success are not always consistent, however. Some have speculated that being introverted is most important to successful study habits, while being extroverted is valuable in gaining practice through interaction and engaging others in conversation (MacIntyre and Charos, 1996; Dewaele and Furnham, 1999). This is supported by the findings of a number of existing studies.[8] For example, in a recent test of this theory, MacIntyre and Charos (1996) found that level of extroversion is negatively related to language anxiety, and language anxiety is in turn a strong predictor of unwillingness to communicate in the language. Using an assessment of the well-established "Big Five" personality traits, they found positive relationships not only with extroversion but also with the other four traits.[9] Specifically, agreeableness showed a small but significant positive relationship with willingness to communicate; openness to experience (also called intellect) was related to perceptions about one's own competence in the language; emotional stability was related to willingness to interact with members of the second-language community; and conscientiousness was related to positive attitudes toward the language-learning situation. Overall, these findings suggest that excluding people who are unsuccessful at language learning may change the personality characteristics of the officer force but the nature of the potential changes is not yet fully understood.

---

[7] For examples of the usage of this term, see Schumann, 1975, MacIntyre and Charos, 1996, and Javad and Noordin, 2011.

[8] See Dewaele and Furnham, 1999, for a review.

[9] The "Big Five" is a well-established model for understanding and measuring personality (see, for example, Goldberg, 1990).

Knowing More Than One Language

Learning a third or subsequent language differs substantially from learning a second (Kroll, 2010) for a variety of reasons, among them language transfer, metacognition and metalinguistic awareness, and learner autonomy.

Language transfer refers to how a learner's knowledge of his or her current languages influences the learning of a new language. While a majority of studies indicate that transfer facilitates third-language learning, the degree of similarity between the languages is very important (Ringbom, 2007). For example, Corin (1997) reported on a DLI conversion course for second-language speakers of Czech to learn Serbo-Croatian, a similar language. After a three-month period of instruction, the median ILR oral proficiency score for the group was a 2 in Serbo-Croatian. Such successful transfer would not be expected for highly dissimilar languages.

Prior language learning also helps increase metacognition (the learner's ability to think about his or her own learning processes) and metalinguistic awareness (understanding of language as an object and the ability to think about how languages work). Numerous studies have concluded that bilinguals and multilinguals have a higher degree of metalinguistic awareness than monolingual speakers. For example, Jessner (1999) examined problem-solving behavior among bilinguals learning a third language and found that the learning strategies of experienced language learners were different from those of less experienced learners.

Finally, learner autonomy (the tendency or ability to control one's own learning process) tends to be stronger among those who already know two or more languages (Rivers and Golonka, 2009; Klein, 1995). One study of learners at a university and at DLI found that bilinguals learning a third language preferred to control their own learning processes and had a greater tendency to request changes to the course content and structure (Rivers, 1996). These learners were able to master more of the language in a shorter time than monolinguals were, as demonstrated by test performance at the end of the respective courses.

These studies confirm that those who already know two or more languages are generally more successful at learning third or subsequent languages. This suggests that an Air Force officer accession policy that requires all officers to know at least one language other than English is likely to result in a corps of individuals who are better primed for subsequent language learning than those who do not already speak a second language.

Language-Learning Disability

The exact nature of language-learning aptitude is still being debated, but the question of whether a foreign-language learning disability exists is far more controversial. The U.S. government defines a learning disability as

> a disorder in one or more of the basic psychological processes involved in understanding or in using language, spoken or written, that may manifest itself in an imperfect ability to listen, think, speak, read, write, spell, or to do mathematical calculations . . . including conditions such as perceptual disabilities, brain injury, minimal brain dysfunction, dyslexia, and developmental aphasia. (20 USC 1401)

Many academic institutions require second-language courses, and some students claim a foreign-language learning disability in seeking waivers of the requirement. Those who contend that such a disability exists point to the fact that some individuals may score low on language aptitude tests and perform poorly in language courses while demonstrating achievement and high aptitude in other areas (Reed and Stansfield, 2002). However, others argue that there is no empirical evidence of a unique disability for second-language learning, but rather that those who perform poorly at language learning are simply on the continuum that ranges from very strong to very weak language learners (Sparks, 2009). At the moment, the debate continues, but the question may have implications for the Air Force's decisions on a language proficiency requirement because the Air Force would have to consider how best to deal with the uncertainty over this disability, whether to acknowledge it, and whether eliminating those who have it would have any effect on the composition of the officer corps or raise questions of discrimination when compared to past officer accession practices.

Educational Programs Designed to Achieve High Levels of Proficiency

Although many institutions are regarded as leaders in developing language proficiency, we focus here on the DLIFLC and the university language programs funded under the National Security Language Program's Language Flagship Initiative because their curricula are specifically designed to help students reach certain ILR proficiency levels.[10]

DLIFLC provides instruction in 24 languages. According to DLIFLC (2010):

> Education is culturally based, learner-centered and proficiency-oriented, employing authentic speech and materials. . . . Teaching is accomplished within a framework that provides intensive practice and interaction in the target language, as spoken by educated teachers of that language. The student starts with carefully selected texts and structured exercises to practice listening and reading comprehension and speaking, and then moves toward creative use of the language. Throughout the program, emphasis is placed on communicative competence in real-life situations, to include appropriate military terminology. Together with language instruction, DLIFLC's programs also stress cultural and geographical knowledge of the appropriate regions and countries.

The classes for DLIFLC programs take place five days a week, last six to seven hours a day, and require two to three hours of homework each night. They are designed to have students reach at least ILR levels of 2/2/1+. For category IV languages, the basic program requires 64 weeks of study. In comparison, category III languages last 48 weeks, and category I languages last 26 weeks.

The Language Flagship Programs began with initial grants awarded in late 2002 to create university-level programs for advanced language education in languages critical to U.S. competitiveness and security (Language Flagship, 2012). Funded by the National Security Education Program, flagship language programs cover Arabic, Mandarin Chinese, Hindi, Urdu, Korean, Persian, Central Eurasian Turkic languages, Russian languages, and African languages.[11] The programs are designed to enable college students, including those with little to no proficiency in a target language, to achieve superior language proficiency (corresponding to a 3

---

[10] There is a wealth of information on the many approaches to language teaching, including immersion, study abroad, heritage language programs, and others. A review of them is beyond the scope of this report; but Long and Doughty, 2009, is a good starting point for more information on those topics.

[11] See Appendix C for a list of the Language Flagship Programs.

on the ILR scale) in four to five years, while pursuing another major of their choice. On completing the program, participants are required to work for the U.S. government in a position with national security responsibilities for a period equivalent to the duration of assistance they received under the program. The departments of Defense, Homeland Security, and State and agencies of the U.S. Intelligence Community are priority agencies for candidates.

Curricula vary across institutions and languages, but all employ communicative and/or proficiency-oriented teaching approaches with intensive language and culture instruction and overseas immersion. One representative example is the Russian Flagship Program at University of Wisconsin, Madison.[12] For this DLI category III language, the requirements are

- the equivalent of four years of Russian language courses
- a two-semester Russian culture course taught in Russian
- a senior capstone course
- an advanced-level seminar in Russian, with research papers written in Russian on a topic in the student's major discipline
- two Russian area studies courses with a Russian-language component
- individual and small-group tutorials in Russian
- extracurricular activities, including workshops, lectures, films, and social activities
- a year-long overseas program at a university in Russia.

A representative example for Chinese, a DLI category IV (and therefore more demanding) language comes from the Chinese Language Flagship Program at Arizona State University.[13] The requirements for a student beginning with no Chinese language skills are

- the equivalent of four years of Chinese language courses, which may include an intensive summer Chinese language program in China or at an approved U.S. institution
- two courses in advanced Chinese for professional purposes
- a course on a topic related to Chinese culture
- two courses in literary Chinese
- a course in Chinese linguistics
- at least two courses in Chinese literature
- at least two courses in humanities and social sciences related to China
- a capstone year in China during which the student enrolls in content classes taught in Chinese at a Chinese university and completes an internship, functioning as a professional using the Chinese language
- a course in Chinese culture.

These examples reveal the time and investment of resources required to train an individual in one of the more difficult languages. The time required has important implications for an officer accession policy because requiring Air Force officers to achieve a level of 3/3—or even 2/2—would require officer prospects to be willing and able to undertake such rigorous training unless they had already acquired a second language through some other means, such

---

[12] Please see the University of Wisconsin, Madison, websites described in the references for more information on this program.

[13] Please see the Arizona State University website, described in the references, for more information on this program.

as prior study or heritage language exposure. As we will discuss again later, this would have important implications for the pool of potential Air Force officers.

After Language Learning: Attrition and Maintenance

Adult language learners typically exert a great deal of effort to acquire second languages and require continuing effort to maintain them. Unfortunately, many language learners leave their classrooms or immersion experiences only to find that they no longer have the opportunity or need to use the language. Studies have shown that even those who spend years learning a language are almost certain to lose it without continued use. For some, as little as six months of disuse can produce significant amounts of skill loss (Lambert and Freed, 1982; Weltens, 1987).

In light of the potential for degradation of language skills, it is just as vital to identify methods of maintaining languages as to identify methods for language learning. Fortunately, the same factors that determine learning success—aptitude, personality, cultural attitudes, and how the language was learned—can improve maintenance and mitigate loss. Further, many of the same strategies used to learn a language initially can be used to maintain it, including travel abroad, computer-aided instruction, self-instruction, and seeking opportunities in the local and global communities to interact with other speakers of the language (Gleason, 1988).

Therefore, if an Air Force policy were to require all officers to achieve second-language proficiency for commissioning, the Air Force would also need to provide well-designed support for language maintenance to prevent or minimize the loss of language skills.

Implications

Requiring a Second Language Is Likely to Substantially Decrease the Number of Eligible Officer Candidates

Few individuals will start out with the needed linguistic skills, and those who lack them may find acquiring them overly burdensome. The supply of second-language speakers in the United States is limited, so the Air Force must consider whether it is feasible to require officer candidates to undergo language training to be eligible for commissioning.

The training available through DLIFLC and national-security-oriented flagship programs is demanding and time consuming. Existing estimates for the amount of study needed to achieve working proficiency suggest that typical college courses alone cannot be relied on to produce proficiency among students who are not majoring in the language. For highly motivated language learners attending the Foreign Service Institute or DLI, reaching level 2 requires at least a year of intensive, full-time study. Reaching level 3 through the National Security Education Program–sponsored language flagship programs requires at least four years, assuming the language is studied alongside other university coursework. It is important to note that the training for such critically needed languages as Arabic and Chinese requires even more time than would training for languages that are easier for English speakers to learn.

Not Even Training All Candidates Guarantees Success

The ability to learn languages varies greatly. Such individual factors as age, aptitude, motivation, personality, and prior language learning may influence outcomes to varying degrees.

The research on age of acquisition confirms that language-learning success in adults (unlike in children) is not guaranteed. Therefore, policies directed at initiating language-learning efforts in adulthood, such as in college, will not be uniformly successful for all learners. Learners with higher language aptitudes are more likely to be successful, but the Air Force must consider that the effect of screening candidates by either working proficiency (2/2/2) in a second language or language aptitude could substantially reduce the size of the candidate pool. It is also worth noting that the notion of a disability for learning languages remains controversial and is no less so in the context of the military services, where most disabilities are considered criteria for exclusion from service. However, as noted above, if the Air Force were to require second-language study or proficiency, the organization would need to develop a policy for those who might be diagnosed with foreign-language learning disability.

A Requirement Alone Might Not Be Enough to Motivate Learning or Maintenance

Motivation for language learning and maintenance is also a key consideration in establishing a language policy. Research suggests that providing external rewards for language learning and maintenance can help, but some degree of intrinsic motivation is important. What creates such intrinsic motivation and whether it can be enhanced through policies have yet to be determined, but it is unlikely that extrinsic incentives alone, such as foreign-language bonus pay, would be sufficient to motivate officers to acquire and maintain second-language skills.

Requiring a Second Language Could, However, Produce Some of the Desired Benefits

Because success at learning a language is generally associated with some degree of acculturation, and language learning is often associated with positive changes in attitudes toward other cultures, it stands to reason that a language requirement could have the secondary consequence of creating an officer corps with a higher degree of cultural openness. Furthermore, those who know two or more languages tend to be better language learners than those who do not know a second language. This suggests that a second-language requirement would likely result in a corps of individuals who are more primed for subsequent language learning than those who speak only one language.

The Requirement Would Most Likely Change Officer Corps Demographics

Policies that directly or indirectly eliminate people who do not know (or acquire) a second language will likely change the demographics of the Air Force. Recruiting those who are more likely to already be proficient in a second language may mean drawing more heavily from among heritage speakers, foreign-language majors, and individuals who received their early education in urban areas, which are likely to have schools with foreign-language classes. In addition, certain personality traits (such as introversion) may be associated with greater success, and individual aptitudes for language vary greatly. The precise nature of the demographic changes is not yet certain, but the potential changes should be weighed and scrutinized carefully to be sure none are detrimental.[14]

---

[14] As noted earlier, selecting only people who are proficient at a 2/2 or higher could yield a more homogeneous group of officers with respect to personality. Given that personality is related to other workplace outcomes, including apparently unrelated aspects of job performance, the relationships between language proficiency and personality need to be better understood to keep a foreign-language proficiency policy from having unintended detrimental effects on other important workplace outcomes.

CHAPTER THREE

Survey of Air Force Officers

We surveyed current Air Force officers to examine many of the key issues related to a language requirement. Other types of studies and data collection efforts, such as educational experiments, in-depth language assessment, and focus groups and interviews, would be useful supplements to this investigation.

The survey allowed us to take an exploratory approach to the issues and cover in detail a wide variety of topics that we believed could be relevant to decisions about Air Force officer accession language policy. We worked from the broad questions stated previously to formulate the following specific research questions, then designed the survey to address them:

- What language skills do current Air Force officers possess?
- Which types of language learning experiences are associated with the highest levels of language skills?
- Are there positive relationships between language skills and various desirable outcomes?
- How would language learning and mandatory language proficiency policies be perceived by officers?
- What do officers perceive as incentives and disincentives for learning a language?

Survey Sample

A total of 12,440 Air Force officers were emailed an invitation to participate in our survey. Approximately 7 percent of the email invitations bounced back with error messages indicating that the email had not been delivered. This resulted in a total of approximately 11,500 valid email invitations. Of those who received valid emails, around 30 percent (a total of 3,519) logged in and completed the entire survey.

The number of individuals invited to take the survey was based on a complex stratified sampling plan using two criteria: language proficiency and commissioned years of service (CYOS).[1] Language proficiency was broken into the following three categories:

1. listening DLPT scores of 0+ or higher in at least one language
2. no listening DLPT score of 0+ or higher but self-assessed proficiency of 3 (fair—understands some words and phrases) or higher in at least one language

---

[1] We used existing archival personnel records of officer's DLPT scores and self-assessed language proficiencies (both of which are included in the personnel record keeping system) to separate people into these stratification categories.

3. no listening DLPT score of 0+ or higher and no self-assessed proficiency of 3 or higher in any language.

For CYOS, we considered each year (less than 1 through 20) separately. From each of the three language proficiency groups and the groups with three or more CYOS, we selected a random sample of 110 people to allow for email bounce-backs (estimated to be 10 percent) and a response rate of approximately 30 percent. Given these estimates, we expected to have approximately 30 respondents in each stratified group.

To ensure stable estimates of the various types of language learning in today's college classrooms, we invited up to 1,600 recently commissioned officers (i.e., those with less than one, one, and two CYOS) from each language proficiency group. Because the entire population of the those falling in proficiency categories 1 and 2 numbered fewer than 1,600 individuals, we invited everyone in these two categories to participate.

Within each stratified group (i.e., within each year of service and in each of the three language proficiency categories), we randomly sampled the prespecified number of individuals just described. The purpose of sampling randomly within each stratum was to ensure that the sample would be representative of that stratum. To account for oversampling (sampling disproportionate to the population size for that group) and differences in actual response rates, we computed response weights by dividing the population of that group by the number of respondents in it. These weights were designed to correct for the sample size differences that result from our disproportionate sampling of and variations in response rates across strata. Applying such corrections allowed us to provide statistical estimates representative of the actual population of officers as a whole. If we had not applied such corrections, the oversampled groups would have influenced the resulting estimates too heavily, making them unrepresentative of the entire officer population.

The weights were applied in any statistical analyses intended to be representative of Air Force officers in general.[2] Table 3.1 shows each stratified group's population size, sample size, and total number of respondents.

Survey Content

The length and content of our survey varied depending on a respondent's answers at various points. Those with no language experiences received fewer follow-up questions than those who had some or many language experiences. All respondents received questions in the following four areas: demographics, attitudes and opinions, language skills, and modes of language acquisition. Each area is described below, and Appendix D contains detailed screen shots of one path through the survey.

---

[2] The majority of the results that were not weighted were correlations. When reporting correlations, we were attempting to describe what the relationship would look like among a group of people who have the full range of scores being correlated. This is more closely aligned with how our unweighted sample was distributed (recall that we invited nearly everyone with DLPT scores of 0+ or higher and basically equal numbers of those reporting fair or better on the self-assessment and people meeting neither criteria) than with how the Air Force officer population is distributed (i.e., most meet neither criteria). Using people who are more evenly distributed across the scale of proficiency (from low to high) permits a better estimate of a hypothetical "true relationship." In all other instances of unweighted results, we are describing our sample of respondents rather than providing an estimate of the Air Force officer population.

Demographics

Several demographic variables were collected during the survey; these included age, college majors and minors, grade point averages, and years of graduation. Other demographic variables, such as CYOS, were merged from existing personnel archives.

Attitudes and Opinions

The most successful policies are those that are well received and that address the concerns of those affected. Therefore, we designed a number of largely exploratory items to measure officers' views about languages, cultures, language learning, and aspects of language policies that the Air Force could implement, such as incentives for and concerns about learning languages and whether a language requirement would have deterred them from joining the Air Force. The exact wording of these items is discussed in detail in Chapter Four.

Language Skills

The most accurate way to assess language skills is through a series of oral and written exams; however, testing each participant in our survey was not feasible. Besides time and resource constraints, the potential variety of languages involved would have required additional tests and testers and would likely have included languages for which valid testing materials would be difficult to obtain.

A second option we considered was using DLPT scores from personnel files, but this presented other issues because the data would not necessarily be complete. Although some officers have DLPT scores on record in existing Air Force personnel files, the number who have such scores is small, and those who do are not representative of officers in general but rather a self-selected group who (a) believe, a priori, that they are likely to meet or exceed the minimum scores for the Foreign Language Proficiency Bonus (the only incentive for taking the test) and (b) are willing to disclose to the military that they are capable in that language. Therefore, using existing DLPT records was also not a viable option. Instead, we opted to use a series of self-assessments to evaluate our respondents' language skills.[3]

We began with a short, nine-point scale to quickly assess people's skills in many languages and route them to appropriate follow-up items in the survey:

0—fewer than ten words
1—about ten to 20 words
2—more than 20 words, but not enough to get around
3—enough to get around, but not enough to have a conversation
4—enough to have a minimal conversation, if speaking slowly
5—able to have simple conversations
6—able to have most everyday conversations with little trouble
7—able to speak easily about some complicated topics
8—at the level of an adult native speaker.

---

[3] Previous studies (such as Clark, 1981) have found certain forms of self-assessments to correlate closely with established formal assessments.

Table 3.1
Population, Sample Size, and Respondents at Each Year of Service (number)

CYOS	DLPT 0+ or higher			Self-Reported as Proficient			Not Language Proficient			Total		
	Population	Sample	Respondents	Population	Sample	Respondents	Population	Sample	Respondents	Population	Sample	Respondents
<1	148	148	61	313	313	133	4,090	1,600	317	4,551	2,061	511
1	162	162	75	373	373	128	3,408	1,600	298	3,943	2,135	501
2	234	234	93	478	478	159	3,507	1,600	284	4,219	2,312	536
3	246	110	48	477	110	33	3,275	110	12	3,998	330	93
4	421	110	41	474	110	25	3,094	110	26	3,989	330	92
5	308	110	47	482	110	30	2,881	110	18	3,671	330	95
6	401	110	51	502	110	34	3,131	110	20	4,034	330	105
7	378	110	44	511	110	27	3,025	110	22	3,914	330	93
8	370	110	37	410	110	39	2,717	110	18	3,497	330	94
9	344	110	54	303	110	40	2,325	110	27	2,972	330	121
10	287	110	49	446	110	26	1,674	110	31	2,407	330	106
11	252	110	53	323	110	51	1,560	110	20	2,135	330	124
12	238	110	43	201	110	43	1,476	110	30	1,915	330	116
13	240	110	45	386	110	36	1,249	110	14	1,875	330	95
14	241	110	54	455	110	38	1,302	110	34	1,998	330	126
15	206	110	48	406	110	45	1,367	110	23	1,979	330	116
16	215	110	50	402	110	35	1,441	110	32	2,058	330	117
17	227	110	57	332	110	41	1,345	110	26	1,904	330	124
18	146	110	47	288	110	38	1,244	110	28	1,678	330	113
19	143	110	47	235	110	39	978	110	28	1,356	330	114
20	102	102	46	175	110	43	812	110	38	1,089	322	127
Total	5,309	2,516	1,090	7,972	3,144	1,083	45,901	6,780	1,346	59,182	12,440	3,519

We asked respondents to use the nine-point scale to report the following for each language:

1. current proficiency in the language
2. highest level of proficiency in the language ever.

We also asked them to indicate their most recent age at best proficiency.

ILR Scale Self-Assessment

We also used a second, deeper self-assessment for more accurate estimates of individuals' ILR skill levels in a subset of languages.

Although proficiency on the ILR scale is best measured via formal testing (as discussed above), Clark (1981) and subsequent studies have established self-assessments in the form of can-do statements as a valid method of collecting language proficiency data for low-stakes purposes. The ILR has published a set of self-assessments with separate measures for speaking, reading, and listening. Each one comprises a series of "can-do" statements describing increasingly sophisticated language performance that are intended to map directly onto the ILR scale. We obtained permission to use the ILR self-assessment in this study and modified it to suit our study's needs.[4]

To estimate participants' ILR skill level, we created a modified version of an existing ILR self-assessment tool (see Appendix B for the modified version). Our modifications reduced the total number of items that respondents had to answer, made the items shorter and clearer, eliminated obscure terms and vocabulary not suitable for lay users, and removed items that seemed less important for defining that skill level. We chose to retain more of the original content of the speaking assessment because this skill area is the most fundamental of the three skills for communicating with others. See Appendix A for a detailed description of each level of speaking, listening, and reading proficiency on the ILR scales and Appendix B for the individual items on our modified ILR self-assessment.

Modes of Language Acquisition

We asked all respondents who knew at least one language other than English to indicate how they had learned the language. For those who knew multiple languages, we asked the question only about the three languages they knew best. Respondents were presented the following options and asked to check all that apply, as well as an opportunity for write-in responses:

- learned it at home as my native language
- learned it at home as one of two or more primary languages in my family
- learned it at home from family members, but it is not my first language
- from a caretaker (e.g., nanny)
- from friends
- extracurricular classes and/or activities with my ethnic, heritage, religious, or cultural community
- courses in elementary school (including extracurricular summer classes)
- courses in junior high or middle school (including extracurricular summer classes)
- courses in high school (including extracurricular summer classes)

---

[4] See ILR, 2001f, 2001g, and 2001h for the unmodified versions.

- college classroom courses (including the U.S. Air Force Academy [USAFA] or any other college or university)
- lived and/or worked in a country where the language is spoken
- private tutor (not paid for by employer, military, or part of my college or high, middle, or elementary school education)
- commercial language school (not paid for by an employer or the military or as part of my college or high, middle, or elementary school education)
- books, computer-based programs, or tapes (not paid for by employer, military, or part of my college or high, middle, or elementary school education)
- study abroad program
- DLI-provided training (including any DLI resource)
- other training provided by the military (not from DLI or USAFA)
- a nonmilitary employer provided training
- other (please specify).

Depending on their responses, we presented follow-up items for up to three languages that included questions on the types and quantity of college or high school courses, the types of DLI training, experiences during study abroad or while working or living abroad, etc. For all languages (up to a total of 12), we also asked respondents to indicate the age at which they first started learning the language.

CHAPTER FOUR

Survey Results

This chapter presents the data analyses and major findings of the survey. To organize and simplify the results, we have grouped them according to the narrow research questions described in Chapter Three. To maintain consistency across figures and to facilitate ease of interpretation for readers, we also standardized the manner in which the results were displayed by computing the findings for four different groups defined by two characteristics of the respondents: CYOS and language skills.[1]

We separated our respondents into two CYOS groups: those commissioned in the last three years and those commissioned more than three years ago. This allowed us to examine responses from individuals most similar to the officers being commissioned now and to report the results for more experienced officers. Where our analyses showed statistically significant and meaningful differences by CYOS, we discuss the findings.[2]

Because the key policy question is about establishing a commissioning requirement for a language proficiency of 2/2 or higher, we also grouped people into the following two language proficiency groups: those with a proficiency of at least a 1+ to 2 or higher on our ILR self-assessment speaking scale and those who have not reached that level in any language on our ILR speaking scale.[3]

The majority of the results are statistically weighted to reflect the subgroup in question. Results not statistically weighted are so noted.[4] For more information on the statistical weighting, see Chapter Three.

---

[1] Maintaining the same display formats allows the reader to examine the same comparisons across research questions, regardless of whether the comparisons were significant on any one research question. Results are not presented separately for all four groups in instances where the sample sizes are small and hence results would not be reliable.

[2] Because our samples were often quite large, many differences are statistically significant, even when the difference is not large enough to be of practical relevance. For this reason, we highlight only differences that are both significant and meaningful. Differences were considered meaningful when they showed a consistent pattern (such as increasing as the level of language skill increased) and when the differences were big enough to provide a sound justification for how to redesign Air Force policy to make it more successful.

[3] Note that we did not distinguish between the 1+ and 2 levels on the ILR. Although the ILR scale is designed around whole-number scoring, most individuals actually fall between levels. Our scoring of the modified ILR self-assessment reflects this fact, and we have grouped people into 1+ or 2+ levels for our analyses. Those at the 1+ levels are closest to the 2/2 level in the proposed policy; hence, our suggestions regarding a 2/2 policy focus on the results for those at the 1+ levels. Therefore, we opted to use the cut point of 1+ or higher for splitting out analyses. For additional information about the ILR language scale, see the section on the ILR scale in Chapter Three and the results reported below, in the section titled "Language Skills Among Air Force Officers."

[4] The majority of the results that were not weighted were correlations. When reporting correlations, we were attempting to describe what the relationship would look like among a group of people having the full range of scores being correlated. This is more closely aligned with how our unweighted sample was distributed (recall that we invited nearly everyone with

As a preview and for reference purposes, Table 4.1 summarizes the key findings and implications and identifies the pages that discuss these topics.

Language Skills Among Air Force Officers

We considered three different aspects of officers' language skills: skill level, number of languages, and which languages.

Proficiency

As described in Chapter Three, we asked survey respondents to self-report their current and best-ever proficiency levels for every language of which they have ever known at least ten words (Figures 4.1 through 4.3).

Table 4.2 shows that none of the measures of language skills are related to CYOS and that all the language skill measures are significantly related to one another. Although the strong relationships were not surprising, this finding led us to conclude that it would be redundant to report results separately for speaking, reading, and listening. Consequently, as speaking represents a key component of effective communication with foreigners and in many settings the most useful skill set of the three, we opted to present results for speaking only from here forward.[5]

Figure 4.1 shows that, on the whole, officers' proficiency levels permit only limited interactions in a second language. For example, approximately 21 percent of the recently commissioned officers reported an ILR self-assessment score below a 0+. Also, as shown in Table 4.1, the average current proficiency in the language they reported as knowing best is just over a 3 on our nine-point scale, or "enough to get around, but not enough to have a conversation." This level is consistent with the average self-reported ILR self-assessment scores on reading, listening, and speaking shown in Table 4.1, which correspond to ILR proficiencies in the 1 to 1+ range.[6]

Although Figure 4.1 confirms that the majority of officers have very limited language skills and that about 15 percent of recently commissioned Air Force officers reported speaking a second language at a level of 3+ or higher, Table 4.1 and Figure 4.1 also show that the mean for best-ever proficiency is noticeably and significantly higher than the mean for current proficiency. This suggests that officers typically do not maintain their skills at highest proficiency. This finding also suggests that efforts to commission officers with proficiencies of 2/2 or higher will not necessarily result in officers with skills at that level later in their careers. Additional efforts would need to be directed at maintaining those same levels of skills after commissioning.

DLPT scores of 0+ or higher and basically equal numbers of those reporting fair or better on the self-assessment and people meeting neither criteria) than with how the Air Force officer population is distributed (i.e., most meet neither criteria). Using people who are more evenly distributed across the scale of proficiency (from low to high) permits a better estimate of a hypothetical "true relationship." In all other instances of unweighted results, we are describing our sample of respondents rather than providing an estimate of the Air Force officer population.

[5]   While speaking is a key element of communicating with foreigners, reading or listening skills may be just as, or even more, important in other aspects of military work (e.g., intelligence). Our decision to use speaking throughout the results is not intended to diminish this fact.

[6]   Individuals at level 1 can offer basic courtesy and conduct simple face-to-face conversations on familiar topics. Those at level 1+ can initiate and maintain predictable face-to-face conversations and satisfy limited social demands.

Table 4.1
Overview of Survey Findings

Research Question	Key Survey Findings	Policy Implications	See Pages
What language skills do current Air Force officers possess?	The average skill level is in the elementary proficiency category, with most individuals between 0+ and 2 on the ILR scale.	Most would not meet a 2/2 requirement and would require additional training to do so.	24, 27–28
	The average number of languages (in which they have ever known 10 words or more) is two.	Current officers do have some exposure to multiple languages.	27, 29
	Individuals most often learned languages in school (6th through 12th grades and college); by living and/or working in the country; and through friends, family, heritage communities, and self-study.	Most respondents had taken language courses in school; however, a single type of learning opportunity is not likely to work for all participants.	29, 32–35
	Self-reported best-ever proficiency was significantly higher than current proficiency.	Even officers commissioned at 2/2 needed support to maintain their skills, which diminish otherwise.	24, 27–28
	Seventy-four percent reported Spanish, French, or German as their best language.	More-strategic languages are needed.	28–31
	About one-half of those who did not major in engineering and one-quarter of those who did were required to take a language in college.	The proposed requirement would affect engineers more than other majors.	35–36
	The top three motivations for taking language courses in college were intrinsic interest, major requirement, and usefulness in one's career.	Many officers are already intrinsically interested in languages; others may be motivated by external factors.	37
Which language-learning experiences are associated with the highest levels of language skills?	About 80 percent of FLMMs and 40 percent of engineers and other majors are 1+ or higher; But, at most, only 50 percent of FLMMs are 2+ or higher.	If some FLMMs do not meet a 3/3 or a 2/2 requirement, it is unrealistic to expect non-FLMMs to do so.	38–39
	About 80 percent started learning prior to college, most between ages 13 and 17.	It is not unrealistic to expect language study to begin before college.	39–41
	A sizeable proportion reported first learning a second language at age 23 or older.	Language learning could start after commissioning and still result in measurable proficiency for officers later in their careers.	40
	Those with classroom plus immersion experience had higher proficiencies than those with either experience alone; learning from family has the highest of all.	Immersion experiences should be included in language-training programs. Heritage speakers are among those most likely to meet a 2/2 or 3/3 requirement.	41–44
	Those required to study a language in college reached slightly lower levels of proficiency than those who took it voluntarily in college.	Those who would not take a language voluntarily will not get as much out of the training.	42–45
	The average number of college semesters was 1 to 2, with a majority taking zero; those with higher proficiencies tended to have taken more; and those with 5 or more classes were above a 1+.	More college semesters are better, and at least 5 (and probably more) are needed to meet a 2/2 requirement in a category I language. More difficult languages will certainly require more coursework, but an estimate for how much is not possible given that very few of our respondents have experience with those languages.	44–47

Table 4.1—Continued

Research Question	Key Survey Findings	Policy Implications	See Pages
Are there relationships between language skills and other desirable outcomes?	Those with higher proficiency reported more interest in other cultures.	This might be a possible positive outcome of requiring proficiency, although the gains might be small, and policies that do not rely on language proficiency might be more effective.[a]	47–49
	Those with greater skills reported more interest in and likelihood of learning additional languages.	A language requirement could result in more officers who are more interested in and primed for subsequent language learning.[a]	49–51
	There is a slightly higher likelihood of an officer knowing a third language when he or she already knows a second at a 1+ or higher	Requiring a second language could yield more officers who are better prepared to learn a subsequent language.[a]	52–54
How do officers perceive language learning and mandatory proficiency policies?	They viewed languages as relevant to mission success but as far less so to personal career success.	Need to show officers that it is tied to personal career success by including it in reviews and promotions decisions.	55–57
	Most did not agree that all officers should be required to know a language or that a 2/2 should be required for promotion to lieutenant colonel.	Mandatory language proficiency policies would need more buy-in from officers; at present such policies would not be well-received.	55–59
	A clear majority wished there had been more time to study a language during college; would have stayed an extra year in college to study a language if the Air Force paid; and would have been willing to study something other than Spanish, French or German.	Officers are willing to learn strategic languages if the Air Force provides financial support and time.	58–64
	About 15 percent of those with less than a 1+ proficiency believe that a language requirement might have deterred them from joining the Air Force.	A proficiency requirement would have some effect on who decides to apply to the Air Force.	65–66
What are the perceived incentives and disincentives for learning a language?	The highest ranked incentives were • Air Force paying for it • learning during work hours • learning with spouse • attending immersion programs • being assigned to desirable foreign locations.	Promising avenues for increasing language proficiency include • paying for language courses and training materials • making courses available during work hours and ensuring that time is provided to attend • offering classes with spouses and children • offering immersion programs and time to participate.	70–74
	The highest ranked concerns were • having to learn during personal free time • being passed over from promotion because they were not focused on primary work duties • having to spend time away from family • being better off doing other work that supports the mission.	The best avenues for eliminating perceived obstacles to language learning include • providing ample opportunities during work hours for learning and maintenance • factoring efforts to improve and maintain skills into promotion decisions.	70–74

[a] Note that direction of causality for these relationships is unknown. For example, learning a language may have no effect on cultural interest; instead interest in other cultures might cause people to study harder resulting in greater language proficiency. This is an alternative and equally reasonable explanation for the observed relationship. The direction of causality would impact whether the proposed benefits of the policy would be realized.

Figure 4.1
ILR Self-Assessment Scores

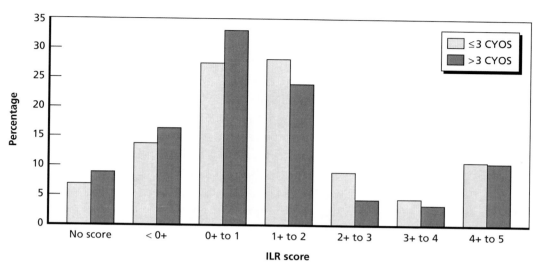

NOTE: Includes the full sample (*n* = 3,519). "No score" refers to those who had not learned ≥10 words in another language.

RAND *TR1189-4.1*

Figure 4.2
Current Language Proficiency Scores

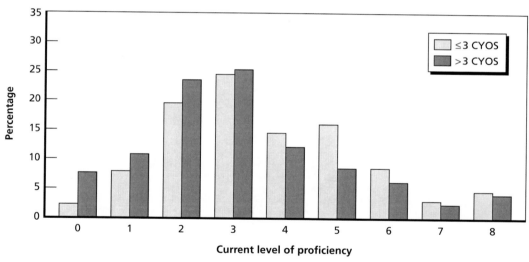

NOTE: Includes only those who have learned ≥10 words in another language (*n* = 3,381).

RAND *TR1189-4.2*

Number of Languages

Figure 4.4 shows that officers know an average of 2.06 languages. Somewhat surprisingly, a majority (more than 60 percent) reported having known more than ten words in two or more languages (other than English), and fewer than 5 percent reported never having known more than ten words in even one. This tells us that current officers do have some exposure to multiple languages other than English.

Figure 4.3
Best-Ever Language Proficiency Scores

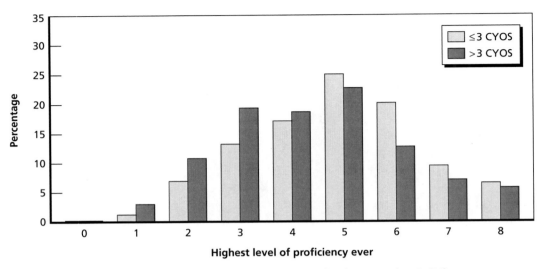

NOTE: Includes only those who have learned ≥10 words in another language (*n* = 3,408).
RAND *TR1189-4.3*

Table 4.2
Weighted Descriptive Statistics and Unweighted Correlations Among Measures of Language Skills

		Mean	Standard Deviation	1	2	3	4	5	6
1	CYOS	7.8	5.7	1.00					
2	Proficiency now	3.2	1.9	0.00	1.00				
3	Best-ever proficiency	4.5	1.7	−0.01	0.87	1.00			
4	ILR score, speaking	1.7	1.4	−0.01	0.71	0.64	1.00		
5	ILR score, listening	1.7	1.5	−0.02	0.68	0.62	0.88	1.00	
6	ILR score, reading	1.5	1.2	−0.01	0.62	0.58	0.80	0.81	1.00

NOTES: The means and standard deviations are weighted to reflect the Air Force officer population. The correlations are not weighted. All correlations greater than 0.10 are significant at *p* <0.01. The ILR Self-Assessment scores and the nine-point self-report scores are not on the same scale, so the means should not be expected to be the same across the measures. Observations for these variables range from 3,384 to 3,519.

Types of Languages

Table 4.3 lists all languages our respondents reported (excluding languages with fewer than five respondents, to protect the anonymity of our participants) and shows the number of respondents for each of three different levels of proficiency. Many people reported knowing multiple languages and are therefore represented in multiple rows. For example, someone who knows

Figure 4.4
Number of Languages in Which Respondents Knew Ten Words or More

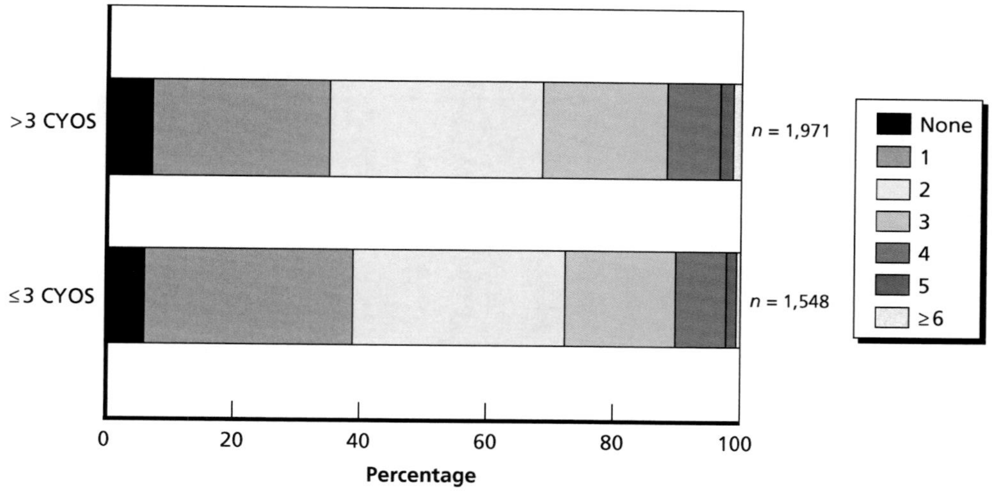

RAND *TR1189-4.4*

Spanish, American Sign Language,[7] and Korean would be counted in the totals for all three languages.

Table 4.4 shows the proportion of those who reported knowing the indicated language best. Unlike the previous table, respondents here were not double counted. For those who reported knowing multiple languages, we counted only the language they selected as their best. Spanish, German, and French top the list, accounting for 74 percent of officers' best languages. Less than 1 percent reported Arabic as their best language. The findings on the languages the officers currently know show that their skills most heavily represent the languages most commonly taught in the United States. These languages, however, are not the ones more critical for national security, such as Arabic and Chinese. Therefore, considering these existing language skills, more individuals who speak strategic languages are still needed.

Although the vast majority of officers indicated that the language they knew best was Spanish, German, or French, our review of the college catalogs at schools with Air Force ROTC detachments showed that about one-half offered courses in Arabic, and more than 75 percent offered courses in Japanese and Chinese. Nevertheless, they offered far fewer courses in these other languages. The median number of courses for Arabic was six, while the medians for Spanish, French, and German were 20, 18, and 13, respectively. For more information on language courses in ROTC schools, see Appendix E.

Methods of Language Learning

Figures 4.5, 4.6, and 4.7 show the proportion of respondents who selected each type of learning experience in the top three languages that respondents know best. These results show that

---

[7]   Our survey included two languages not spoken in other nations: American Sign Language and Latin. While these languages are not of operational use to DoD, we included them because of the proposition that learning any language other than English benefits subsequent language learning (one of the primary arguments promulgated in support of the proposed officer accession language policy). If that is the case, the benefits should generalize to American Sign Language and Latin. Together, they account for only 1.2 percent of the weighted sample for languages our respondents know best (see Table 4.4); hence, their influence on our findings is negligible. For these reasons, we opted not to exclude them from our analyses.

Table 4.3
Types of Languages and Best-Ever Proficiency Levels of Respondents

Language	Proficiency			Total Respondents (unweighted)
	Minimal (0–2)	Moderate (3–5)	High (6–8)	
None[a]				104
Spanish	431	1,227	771	2,442
German	281	628	340	1,255
French	235	594	279	1,112
Japanese	163	209	76	449
Italian	95	246	73	416
Russian	98	151	99	351
Chinese, Mandarin	85	72	87	244
Arabic, Modern Standard	106	84	33	225
Korean	88	64	49	201
Portuguese	30	62	59	152
Latin	46	88	14	150
Tagalog	26	21	68	117
Turkish	30	44	14	88
Hebrew	25	32	15	73
Arabic, Iraqi	45	11	2	58
American Sign Language (ASL)	18	27	11	57
Dutch	8	30	15	54
Thai	14	18	12	44
Greek, Ancient	20	15	6	43
Greek, Modern	15	19	9	43
Persian [Afghan], Dari	21	15	5	41
Polish	10	11	19	40
Vietnamese	3	8	26	37
Chinese, Cantonese	8	8	15	32
Persian [Iranian], Farsi	13	12	6	32
Norwegian	13	7	6	26
Swedish	7	7	9	23
Hindi	4	6	10	20
Swahili	13	5	1	19
Serbo-Croatian	2	9	7	18
Danish	5	6	6	17
Ilocano [Ilokano]	3	4	10	17
Indonesian	2	6	8	16
Ukrainian	4	8	4	16

Table 4.3—Continued

Language	Proficiency			Total Respondents (unweighted)
	Minimal (0–2)	Moderate (3–5)	High (6–8)	
Hungarian	1	5	9	15
Pashto (Pushtu) [Afghan]	9	4	2	15
Egyptian	3	7	2	12
Romanian	3	3	5	11
Urdu	1	2	8	11

[a] Has never known at least ten words in **any** language.

Table 4.4
Language Reported as Highest Level of Proficiency

Language	Weighted Percentage	Total Respondents (unweighted)
<10 words in any language	6.5	104
Spanish	46.5	1,448
French	13.9	438
German	13.6	565
Italian	2.9	86
Japanese	2.7	129
Russian	2.2	112
Hebrew	1.4	20
Latin	1.0	20
Korean	<1.0	63
Tagalog	<1.0	63
Chinese, Mandarin	<1.0	84
Arabic, Modern Standard	<1.0	34
Polish	<1.0	18
Portuguese	<1.0	48
Turkish	<1.0	20
Vietnamese	<1.0	30
American Sign Language (ASL)	<1.0	14
Chinese, Cantonese	<1.0	12
Dutch	<1.0	14
Thai	<1.0	14
Indonesian	<1.0	10
Other[a]	2.8	160
Total	100.0	3,506

[a] All other languages represented less than 1 percent of the officer population per language and had fewer than ten respondents per language.

Figure 4.5
How Respondents Learned Their Best Language

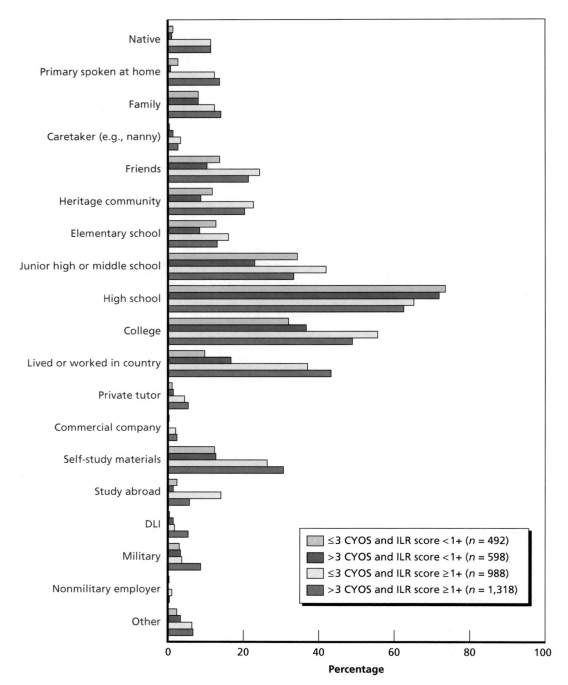

Figure 4.6
How Respondents Learned Their Second-Best Language

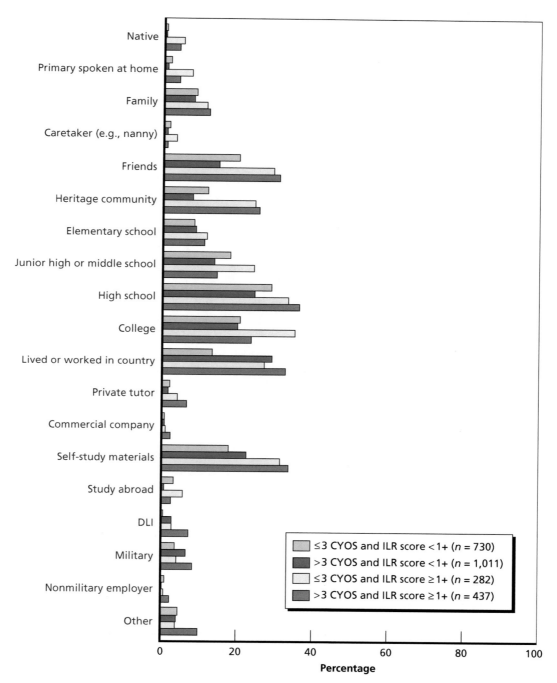

Figure 4.7
How Respondents Learned Their Third-Best Language

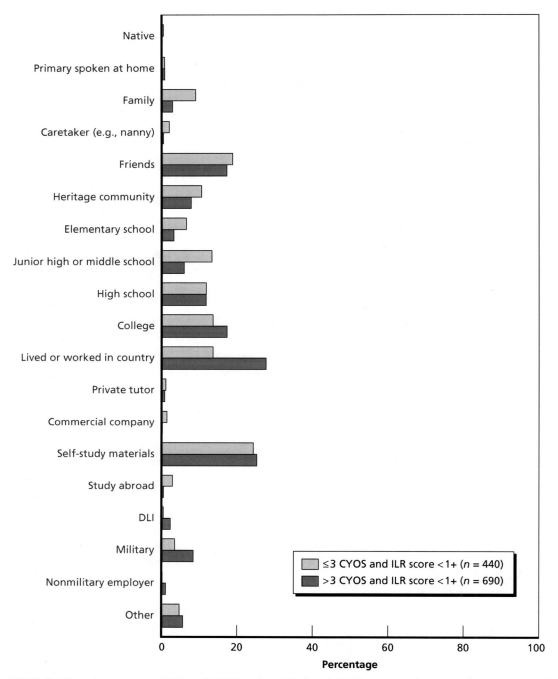

NOTE: For the ≥1+ group, *n* = 36 for ≤3 CYOS and *n* = 72 for >3 CYOS. Because these samples are too small to yield stable estimates, they are not included here.

RAND *TR1189-4.7*

the predominant modes of learning a language include conventional education settings (ranging from junior high or middle school through college), living or working in the country, and self-study materials. Friends, family, and heritage communities also had notable endorsement, particularly among officers with high proficiencies.

Figure 4.5 also shows some interesting differences between those whose skills are 1+ or higher, namely that they tended to be more likely than those who were below a 1+ to endorse nearly all of the categories (high school is a notable exception) and some of the starkest differences can be seen in self-study and lived/worked in country. Nevertheless, for every category that is endorsed by those with a 1+ or higher, it is also endorsed by many people with less than a 1+. This suggests that prescribing experience in any one type of language-learning opportunity cannot be counted on to produce even moderate levels of proficiency across all participants.

Proportion Required to Take a Language

We asked respondents to indicate whether or not they were required to take a language in college. Figure 4.8 compares the results by CYOS for those who attended the USAFA to those who did not, as well as by engineering majors compared to all other majors. The results show that USAFA has a long history of requiring language classes, while about 50 percent of the other colleges and universities do not. The figure also shows that very high proportions of engineers reported having to take a language at USAFA in the past. This requirement, however, seems to have been lifted in the three to four years prior to our survey. For all other universities and colleges, the proportion of nonengineers reporting such a requirement is nearly double that for engineers, and that finding was consistent across all CYOS. Nevertheless, over 20 percent of engineers did report such a requirement. This finding confirms that the majority of Air Force officers with undergraduate engineering degrees were not required to take language courses in college; thus, adding required language courses to the curriculum would be a notable (and potentially burdensome) change.

Primary Motivations for Taking a Language

As shown in Figure 4.9, an overwhelming majority of respondents (70 percent or more for three of the groups) said they took it because of intrinsic interest (interest in the language for its own sake). The next most frequent reason (picked by about half of the respondents) was a requirement for their major, and a third was that they thought it would help their future career. Interestingly, very few chose the Foreign Language Proficiency Bonus as a reason for taking the language in college. This suggests that respondents either were not aware of the incentive or were not viewing that as a motivating factor during college.

The results for second-best language (shown in Figure 4.10) were generally similar to those for the best language, with one exception. Respondents were less likely to indicate that they studied it because it was required by their major.

Overall, these findings reveal that many different motivations, both intrinsic and extrinsic, influenced officers to learn a language. The Air Force could capitalize on the two most frequently endorsed extrinsic motivations by requiring college language courses and tying language proficiency to career outcomes. In addition, the Air Force could explore methods for generating intrinsic interest in learning a language (the most frequently endorsed motivation) with the hope of increasing the amount of coursework officers and officer candidates are willing to pursue.

Figure 4.8
Percentage Required to Take Language in College

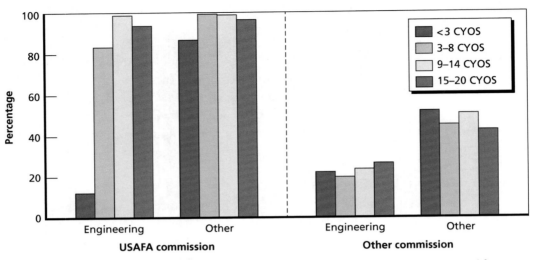

NOTE: This analysis includes 810 USAFA-commissioned officers and 2,630 officers commissioned from another source.
RAND *TR1189-4.8*

Figure 4.9
Reasons for Taking Best Language in College

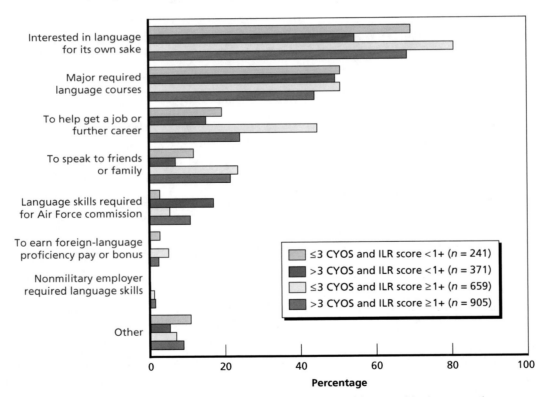

NOTE: Categories may sum to more than 100 percent because respondents could select more than one.
RAND *TR1189-4.9*

Figure 4.10
Reasons for Taking Second-Best Language in College

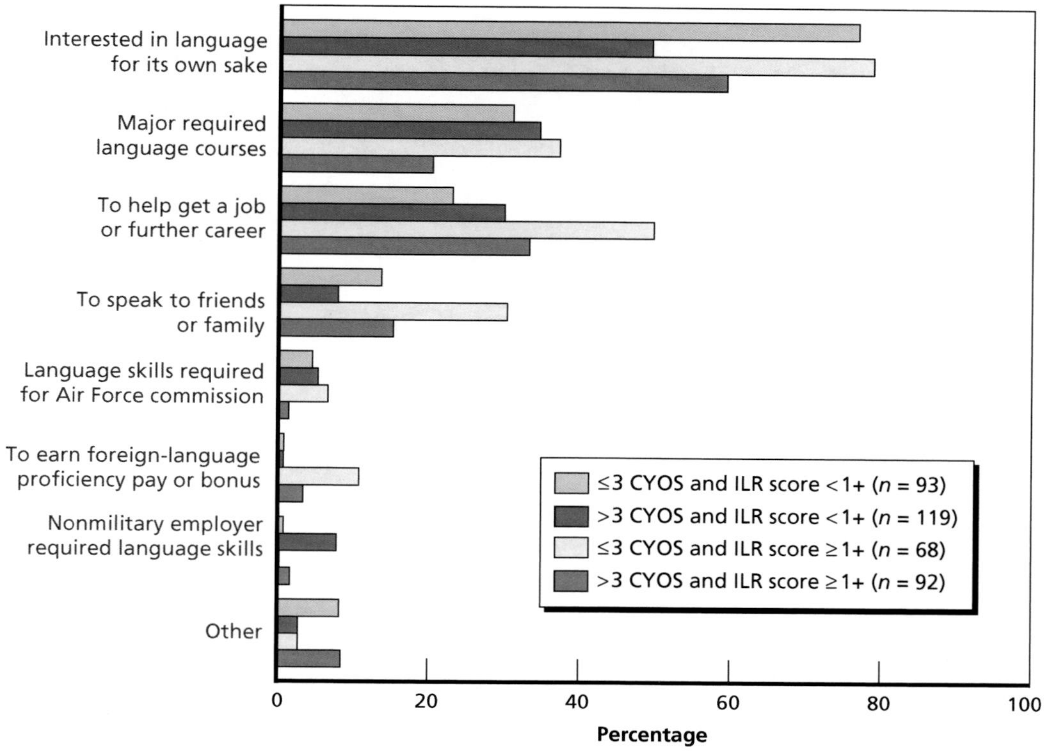

NOTE: Categories may sum to more than 100 percent because respondents could select more than one.
RAND TR1189-4.10

Language-Learning Experiences

Any policy directed at improving officers' language skills should be informed by an understanding of which types of language-learning experiences are most effective and of whether existing language-learning programs tend to produce the desired results. This information will help ensure that resources and efforts are targeted toward the most effective avenues for learning. For that reason, we explored whether the following types of experiences were associated with higher language skill levels:

- majoring in foreign studies rather than engineering or any other subject area
- starting to learn a language at an earlier age
- learning through immersion or via speaking a language at home, as opposed to in a classroom
- whether taking a language in college was voluntary or mandatory
- completing more rather than fewer college courses.

Foreign-Language Majors and Minors, Engineering Majors, and Other Majors

Figure 4.11 compares the ILR self-assessment scores of those respondents who majored or minored in a foreign language or in foreign area studies (foreign-language or foreign-area studies major or minor, FLMM) and those who majored in engineering with those who did not. Figures 4.12 and 4.13 report the proportion of officers in each group with ILR self-assessment scores of 2+ or higher and 1+ or higher, respectively.

As the figures show, FLMMs reported noticeably higher levels of self-reported language skills than non-FLMMs. Specifically, 88 percent of FLMMs who were commissioned within the last three years and 76 percent of FLMMs who were commissioned more than three years ago reported having a current language skill of 1+ or higher on the ILR scale. In stark contrast, fewer than 50 percent of engineers and other non-FLMMs reported knowing a language at a level of 1+ or higher. The finding that engineers' proficiencies were only slightly lower than other non-FLMMs was surprising, given that we assumed that an engineering major's course load is demanding and that engineers would therefore not have the same time to dedicate to language courses.

Very few officers reported skills at 2+ levels or higher. The highest proportions were among FLMMs, but even those were at only 50 percent and 36 percent. Consistent with previous findings, those with greater CYOS tended to report lower levels of language skills.

To determine how much skill is typically attributable solely to college courses, we repeated the comparison between FLMMs and non-FLMMs on the subset of 82 respondents who reported learning their best language in college courses only. Unfortunately, the sample consisted of only ten FLMMs and 16 engineers, making the individual results unreliable. Instead, we combined the engineers and the other non-FLMMs (see Figure 4.14). As the figure shows, the skill levels for the college-only non-FLMM group were noticeably lower than those noted previously for non-FLMMs.

These findings reveal that, even among recently graduated FLMMs, about one-half are not at working proficiency or level 2+ or above. It stands to reason, then, that if FLMMs would

Figure 4.11
ILR Self-Assessment Scores, by Area of Study and CYOS

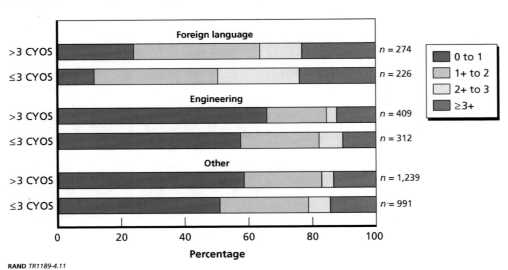

RAND TR1189-4.11

Figure 4.12
Percentage with ILR Self-Assessment Scores of 2+ or Higher, by Area of Study and CYOS

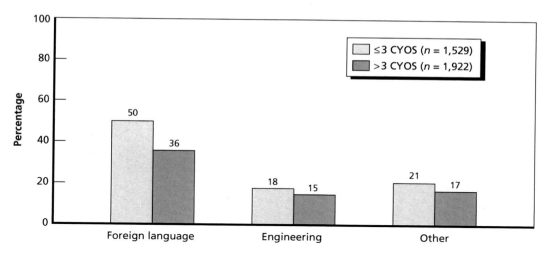

RAND *TR1189-4.12*

Figure 4.13
Percentage with ILR Self-Assessment Scores of 1+ or Higher, by Area of Study and CYOS

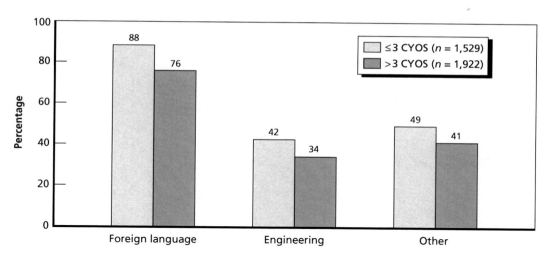

RAND *TR1189-4.13*

not meet a 2/2 requirement, it is unrealistic to expect those who did not major or minor in a language to meet such a requirement.

Age of Acquisition

Of those respondents who took a language in college, an overwhelming majority started learning it long before they entered college. This finding, shown in Figure 4.15, is even more striking for those who did not take the language in college. Many with at least moderate levels of proficiency began learning the language before elementary school. The average age at which respondents began learning foreign languages (Figure 4.16) did not differ much between the

Figure 4.14
ILR Self-Assessment Scores of Non-FLMMs Who Learned Language Only in College Courses

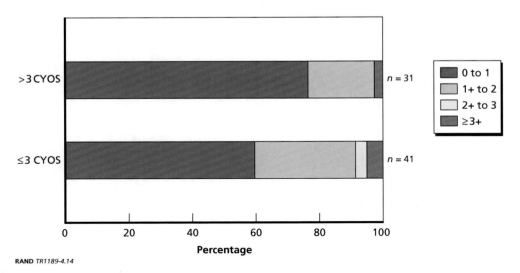

RAND TR1189-4.14

Figure 4.15
Age at Which Language Learning Started: College Versus Noncollege Learners

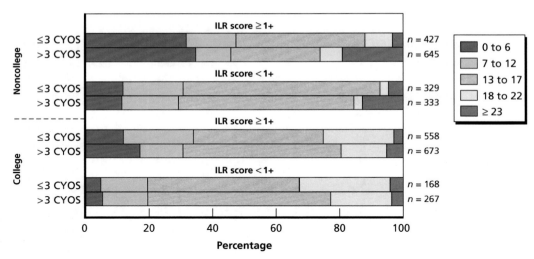

RAND TR1189-4.15

college and not college groups for those who were commissioned more than three years ago. It does, however, differ noticeably for those commissioned in the last three years.

In addition, both figures show that those with an ILR self-assessment of 1+ or higher typically started learning at earlier ages than those with lower proficiencies, although a sizable proportion reported starting to learn the language at age 23 and up.

These findings indicate that language learning could start after commissioning and still produce measurable proficiency for officers later in their careers. However, if the Air Force hopes to have everyone commission at a 2/2 level, officer candidates will need to start learning

Figure 4.16
Average Age at Which Language Learning Started: College Versus Noncollege Learners

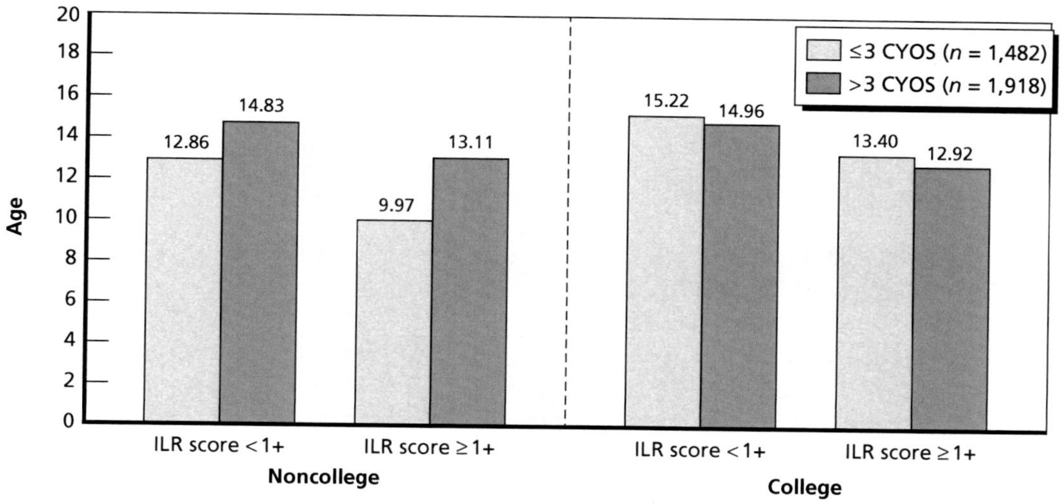

RAND *TR1189-4.16*

the language well before college or will need to spend more time in college on language study, or complete undergraduate language-flagship–like programs.

Figures 4.17, 4.18, and 4.19 show officers' ILR self-assessment proficiencies for those with classroom and/or immersion experience. The classroom experience group includes anyone who took classes in college, high school, middle or junior high school, or elementary school, as well as anyone who received training from a private tutor or has taken classes from a commercial language firm. The immersion group includes only those who had lived or worked abroad or participated in a study abroad program. To help tease apart the effects of classroom training and immersion from other sources of learning, we excluded from the immersion and classroom groups anyone who had learned the language at home from family and instead display results for that group separately (Figure 4.20).

Figures 4.17 through 4.19 clearly show that those with immersion experience tend to have higher proficiencies than those without. While this could suggest that immersion causes higher levels of proficiency, direction of causality cannot be determined from our data. This same relationship between immersion and proficiency could also be observed if students tended to wait until they are at higher levels of proficiency to participate in an immersion experience. Our data do show that those with both immersion and classroom experience tend to have more classroom courses in the language, on average, than those who have classroom experience only. Figures 4.20 and 4.21 show that those who had learned the language at home had much higher proficiencies than those who had not.

These findings suggest that immersion may be an important part of language training for this population.[8] They also confirm that those who learned a language in the home at an early age are more likely to have acquired higher levels of proficiency in a second language prior to commissioning.

---

[8]   There is a wealth of information on the role of immersion in language acquisition. See Cummins, 2009, as a starting point for more information.

Figure 4.17
ILR Self-Assessment Scores for Best Language, Classroom Versus Immersion

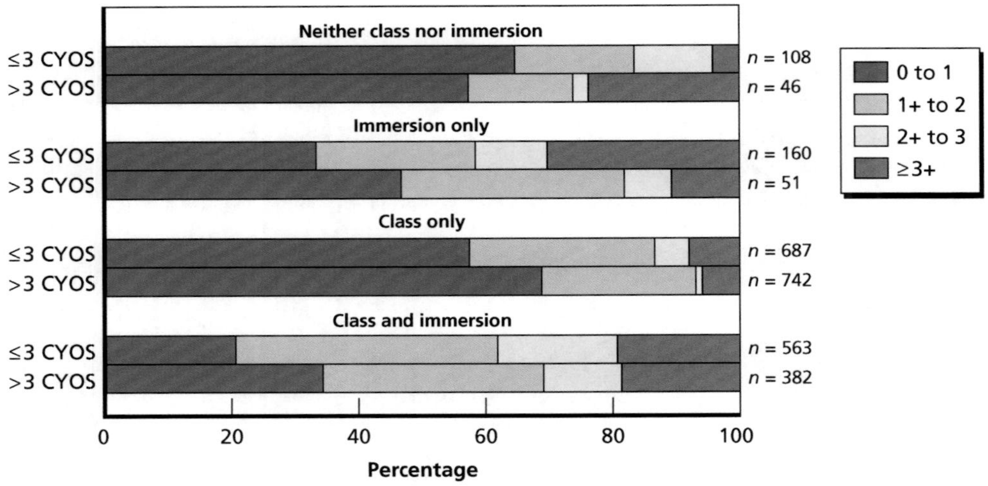

NOTE: Excludes those who learned the language at home.
RAND TR1189-4.17

Figure 4.18
ILR Self-Assessment Scores for Second-Best Language, Classroom Versus Immersion

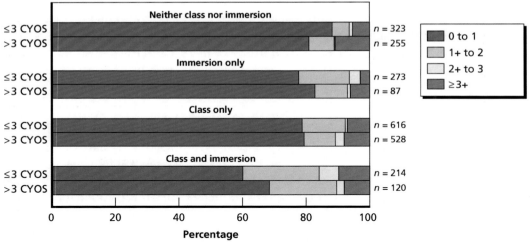

NOTE: Excludes those who learned the language at home.
RAND TR1189-4.18

Voluntary Versus Mandatory College Requirements

One possible policy change for increasing language skills among officers would be to require a specified number of college language courses. Such a policy, however, would assume that those who are forced to take the courses will reap the same benefits as those who would do so voluntarily, which would not necessarily be the case. Because many colleges, universities, and majors do not require students to learn a language as part of their general education requirements, a naturally occurring quasiexperiment was available as part of our survey data. As shown in

Figure 4.19
ILR Self-Assessment Scores for Third-Best Language, Classroom Versus Immersion

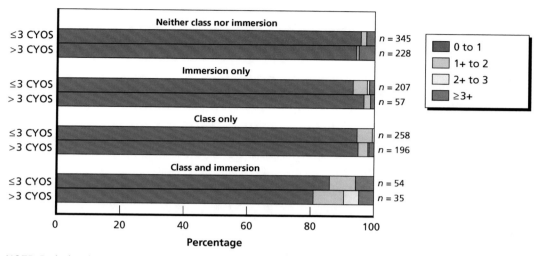

NOTE: Excludes those who learned the language at home.
RAND *TR1189-4.19*

Figure 4.20
ILR Self-Assessment Scores, Those Who Did Versus Those Who Did Not Learn at Home

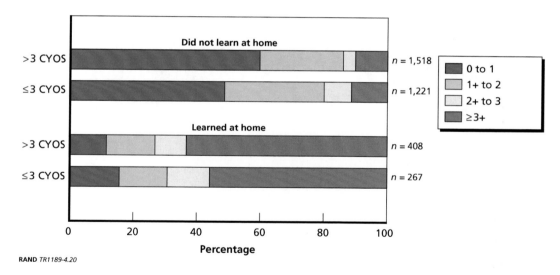

RAND *TR1189-4.20*

Figure 4.22 and Figure 4.23, officers with more than three CYOS who were required to take college language courses reported slightly lower skills than those who were not required to take them. This reveals that those who learned languages voluntarily tended to gain higher levels of proficiency than those who studied language to meet a requirement. This also suggests that a policy that simply requires officers to learn a language might not produce proficiencies as high as one that motivated individuals to do so voluntarily. However, there was very little difference for those who were recently commissioned.

Figure 4.21
Mean ILR Self-Assessment Scores, by Learning Experience

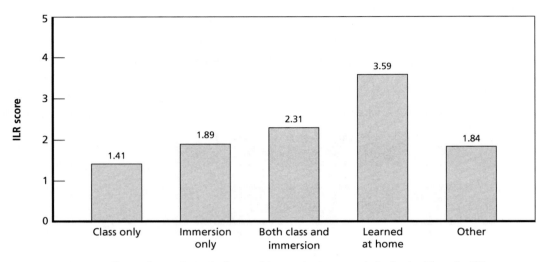

NOTES: n = 3,414. "Class only" and "Both class and immersion" are statistically significantly different from the mean of all the other categories combined.
RAND *TR1189-4.21*

Figure 4.22
ILR Self-Assessment Scores for Mandatory Versus Voluntary Study in College

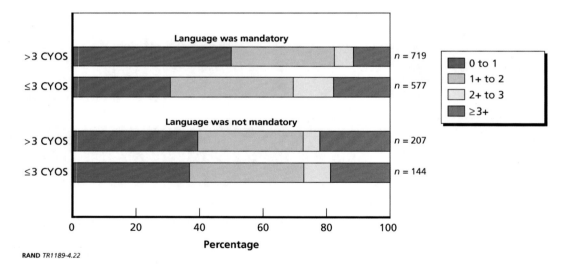

RAND *TR1189-4.22*

Number of College Courses

To determine if there was a relationship between the number of college language courses taken and an officer's ILR self-assessment score, we computed the total number of courses focused on learning to speak, read and understand the language or on reading literature in the original language.[9] To convert the number of courses in the quarter system into semesters, we counted

---

[9]   The survey asked students to list the number of courses they took for five categories of language classes: those focusing on learning to speak, read, and understand the language; those focusing on literature (read in the original language);

Figure 4.23
Mean ILR Self-Assessment Scores for Mandatory Versus Voluntary Study in College

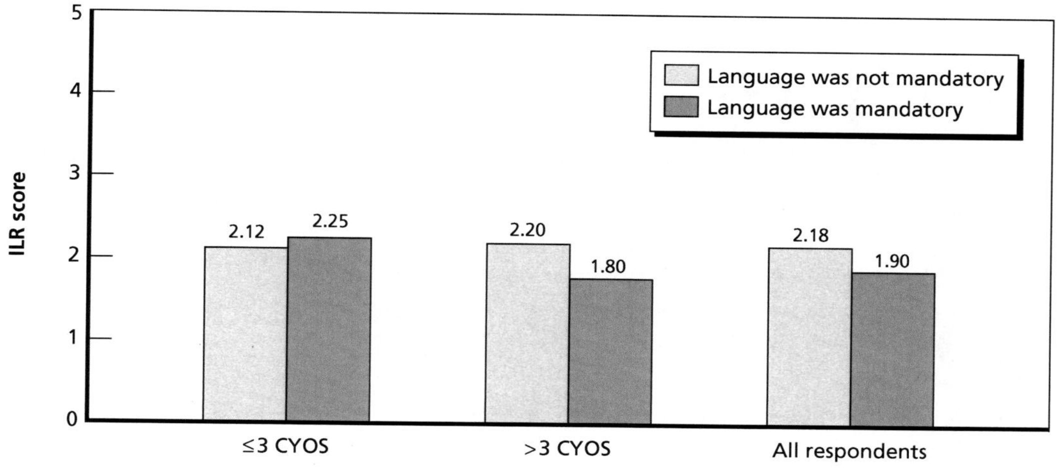

NOTE: This analysis includes 721 officers with ≤3 CYOS and 926 officers with >3 CYOS.
RAND TR1189-4.23

one quarter as two-thirds of one semester (see University of Washington, 2008, for more information on the conversion formula).[10]

Figures 4.24 through 4.27 clearly show that taking three to four semesters of a language does not ensure a language skill level of 1+ or higher; however, those who reported taking five or more courses tended to be much more likely to report skill levels of 1+ or higher. In contrast, those who had taken five to six semesters were almost equally as likely to be below a 2+ as they were to be a 2+ or higher. The figures also show that many of the recently commissioned officers who are below a 1+ have taken multiple semesters of a language. Therefore, if the aim is to get all officers entering the Air Force to a level of 1+ or 2+ or higher, most candidates would need to take at least five to six college semesters for a 1+ skill level or seven to eight for a 2+ skill level, particularly for those who have had no prior language-learning experiences.[11]

---

those focusing on literature (translated to English); those focusing on the history, art, or cultural norms of regions where the language is spoken; and other courses. For these analyses, we included only the courses on learning to speak, read, and understand the language or on literature (read in the original language).

[10] One option on the survey allowed respondents to select "8 or more" courses and about 15 respondents selected the option of "8 or more" *quarters*. When converting quarters to semesters, the "8 or more" response was converted to five to six semesters, then we calculated the results both with and without the 15 responses. We did not see any substantial difference between with and without so we included these responses in the final results. In addition, we counted those who listed a singular quarter, equivalent to two-thirds of a semester, in the one- to two-semester group.

[11] Although the ILR scale is designed around whole-number scoring, most individuals actually fall between levels. As a result, our scoring reflects this fact, and we have grouped people into 1+ or 2+ levels for our analyses. Those at the 1+ levels are closest to the 2/2 level in the proposed policy; hence, our suggestions regarding a 2/2 policy focus on the results for those at the 1+ levels.

Figure 4.24
Semesters of Language Study for Those Scoring ≥1+ and Those Scoring <1+

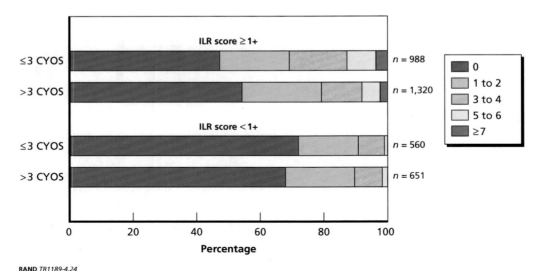

RAND *TR1189-4.24*

Figure 4.25
Semesters of Language Study for Those Scoring ≥2+ and Those Scoring <2+

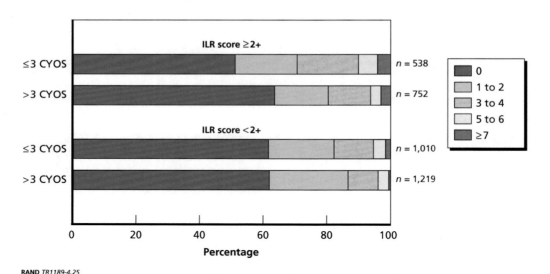

RAND *TR1189-4.25*

Potential Benefits

In discussing the increasing emphasis on language skill development for military service personnel, decisionmakers often consider a range of potential beneficial outcomes beyond the ability to communicate with speakers of another language. Examples of such benefits include an increased desire and capability to learn new languages and increased interest in and tolerance of other cultures. Therefore, we included several items in our survey to further explore these potential benefits. We discuss the results for each below.

Figure 4.26
Mean Number of Semesters of Language Study for Those Scoring ≥1+ and Those Scoring <1+

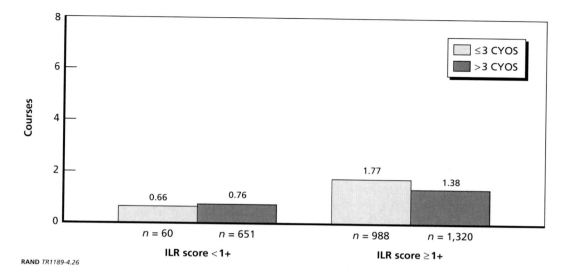

RAND *TR1189-4.26*

Figure 4.27
Mean Number of Semesters of Language Study for Those Scoring ≥2+ and Those Scoring <2+

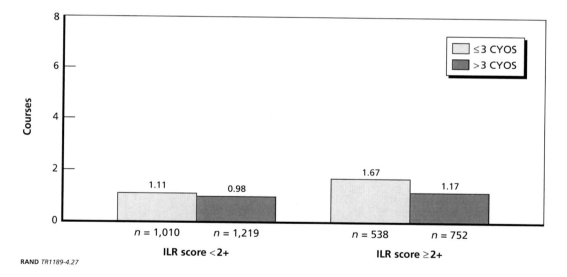

RAND *TR1189-4.27*

Interest in Other Cultures

One often-hypothesized beneficial outcome of learning languages is greater tolerance for, sensitivity to, and interest in other cultures. We, therefore, included the following six survey items:

- I do not feel comfortable with people from other cultures
- It is hard to relate to people from other countries
- I enjoy talking with people from other countries
- I am interested in other people's cultures

- I have a hard time understanding people with foreign accents
- I don't really like people who do not speak English.

Respondents indicated their level of agreement with each item on a seven-point scale ranging from 1 = strongly disagree to 7 = strongly agree. Responses were averaged to produce a total score for interest in other cultures.[12]

Figures 4.28 and 4.29 show that language proficiency is statistically significantly related to interest in other cultures. The unweighted relationships for ILR self-assessment scores and best-ever proficiency with the tolerance for other cultures scale are $r = 0.27$ and 0.29, respectively. Nevertheless, even those who reported never knowing ten words or more in another language do tend to express a positive tolerance for other cultures. Given this positive tolerance from everyone, it is particularly noteworthy that we did, in fact, observe a difference in people's responses to this scale.

Our findings that tolerance and interest are associated with language proficiency could suggest that learning a language could change one's attitudes toward other cultures, but our data cannot say for certain whether such a change would result directly from learning a language. The direction of causality could be the reverse, where being more tolerant of and interested in other cultures could make a person more likely to learn a language and to be successful at it. Nevertheless, one implication is clear: Screening out those who have never learned even a small amount in any other language would eliminate a group that reported, on average, the least positive attitudes toward other cultures.

Figure 4.28
Interest in Other Cultures, by CYOS and ILR Self-Assessment Score

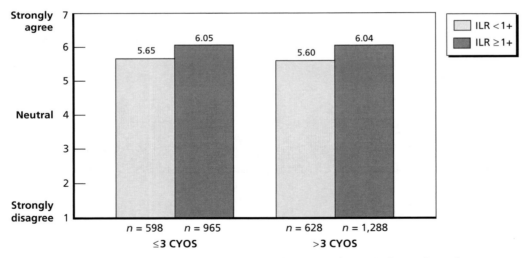

NOTE: Scores were averaged across "I do not feel comfortable with people from other cultures," "It is hard to relate to people from other countries," "I enjoy talking with people from other countries," "I am interested in other people's cultures," "I have a hard time understanding people with foreign accents," and "I don't really like people who do not speak English."
RAND TR1189-4.28

---

[12] Negatively worded responses were reversed before averaging. Note that, in the figures, average scores are continuous; however, for this figure group, 1.00–1.99 = strongly disagree, 2.00–3.49 = disagree, 3.50–4.49 = neutral, 4.50–5.99 = agree, 6.00–7.00 = strongly agree.

Figure 4.29
Average Interest in Other Cultures, by Best-Ever Proficiency

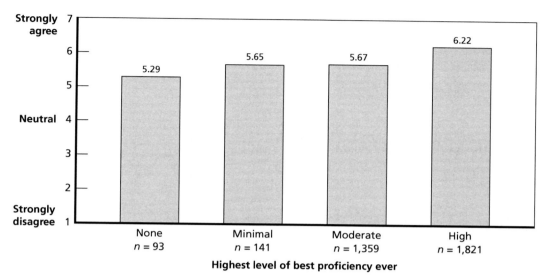

NOTE: Scores were averaged across "I do not feel comfortable with people from other cultures," "It is hard to relate to people from other countries," "I enjoy talking with people from other countries," "I am interested in other people's cultures," "I have a hard time understanding people with foreign accents," and "I don't really like people who do not speak English."

RAND TR1189-4.29

Interest in and LIkelihood of Learning Additional Languages

To test whether learning a language is associated with an increased desire to learn another language, we asked respondents to rate their interest in and likelihood of learning another language in the next five years. The results in Figures 4.30 and 4.31 show that there are substantial and statistically significant differences by language proficiency. More than 50 percent of those who, at some point in the past, knew a language at a level of 6 or higher on our nine-point scale said they had a high level of interest in learning another language in the next five years. Only 7 percent of those who have never known even ten words of a language expressed a similarly strong interest.

The results for the likelihood of learning another language in the next five years showed similar significant differences by proficiency level (Figures 4.32 and 4.33). However, officers were slightly less optimistic about this likelihood than they were for interest, with 31 percent of those with high proficiency and 75 percent of those with no proficiency saying they were not even moderately likely do so. These findings add to what we know from the research literature (that those who know a second language tend to be better at learning subsequent languages) by revealing that, among the survey respondents, those who already knew a second language tended to be substantially more interested in learning another language. This suggests that a language requirement could produce one of the policy's desired effects, priming officers and interesting them in learning another language. However, the results for the likelihood of learning another language suggest that the Air Force would need to explore and address the factors that would prevent officers from following through on their interest.

Figure 4.30
Interest in Learning Another Language, by ILR Self-Assessment Score

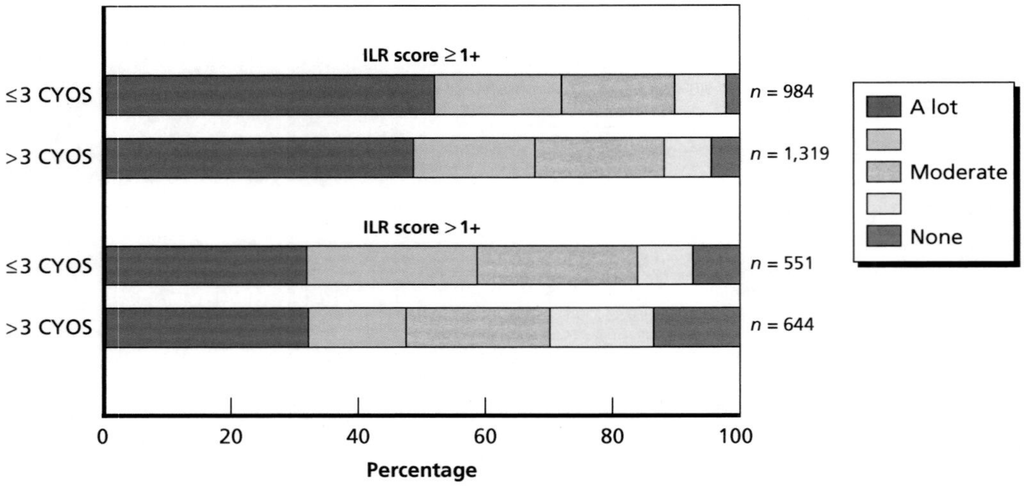

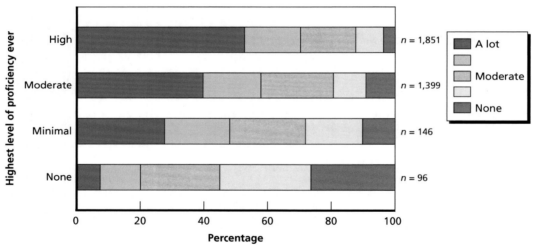

RAND *TR1189-4.30*

Figure 4.31
Interest in Learning Another Language, by Best-Ever Proficiency

RAND *TR1189-4.31*

Self-Efficacy and DLAB Scores

Increased capability to learn another language has been documented in some studies (Corin, 1994; Jessner, 1999). Therefore, we examined two aspects of increased capability in this study: self-perception of ability and ability as measured by the DLAB. The following three items measured self-efficacy (self-perceptions of how good they are at learning languages):[13]

---

[13] Self-perception of one's capability is referred to in the psychological literature as *self-efficacy*, and self-efficacy alone can have meaningful effects on one's success at learning a new skill (for more information, see Bandura, 1997).

Figure 4.32
Likelihood of Learning Another Language, by ILR Self-Assessment Score

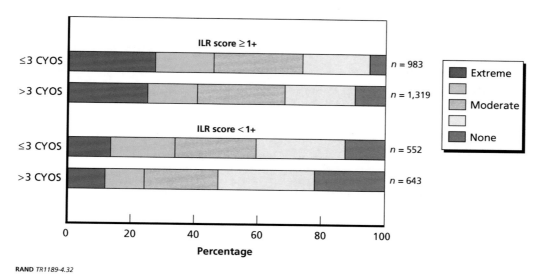

RAND TR1189-4.32

Figure 4.33
Likelihood of Learning Another Language, by Best-Ever Proficiency

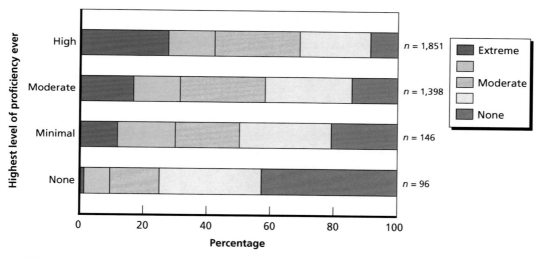

RAND TR1189-4.33

- I have always been good at learning languages.
- I am good at learning new languages.
- Learning languages has always been a challenge for me.

We averaged the responses, which ranged from strongly disagree to strongly agree, to create an overall estimate of self-efficacy (Figure 4.34). We also examined existing DLAB

Figure 4.34
Self-Perceptions of Language-Learning Ability, by ILR Self-Assessment Score

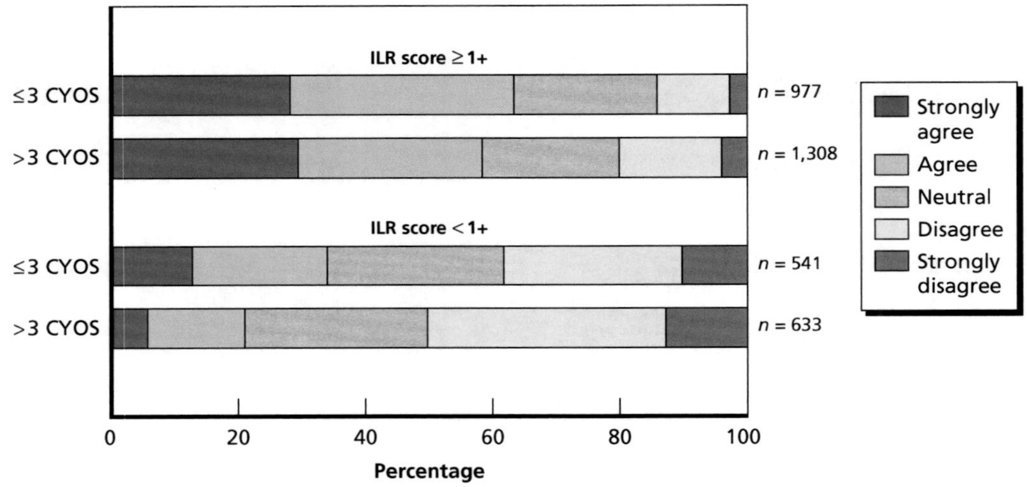

NOTE: Scores were averaged across three survey items: "I have always been good at learning languages," "I am good at learning new languages," and "Learning languages has always been a challenge for me."

RAND *TR1189-4.34*

scores for the small subset of respondents who had taken it within one year of the survey.[14] For context, DLAB minimums for entry into language-intensive careers are 95, 100, 105, and 110 for category I through category IV languages, respectively (see AFI 16-109, 2010). DLAB scores can range from 12 to 164. Figures 4.35 through 4.37 show that language proficiency has a positive relationship with both self-efficacy and DLAB scores. This indicates that those who had already learned a second language also perceived themselves as better language learners and were reasonably accurate at assessing their own language-learning ability.

Although these results do not indicate the direction of causality (e.g., self-efficacy could cause people to be more successful at learning languages, or being successful could cause someone to have high self-efficacy for learning languages), the Air Force could incorporate efforts to increase language learner self-efficacy into its language-learning programs in hopes that this would, in turn, influence the speed and ease with which officers acquire new languages.

Likelihood of Knowing Additional Languages Given Knowing a Second

Although our data cannot tell us how quickly or easily our officers learned additional languages, we did include questions in the survey that would allow us to examine the likelihood that they knew additional languages. More specifically, we evaluated the following two questions:

- Does level of proficiency in a second language affect the likelihood of knowing a third language?

---

[14] Because DLAB scores are considered valid for only one year after testing, we included only scores dated within one year before the survey administration.

Figure 4.35
Self-Perceptions of Language-Learning Ability, by Best-Ever Proficiency

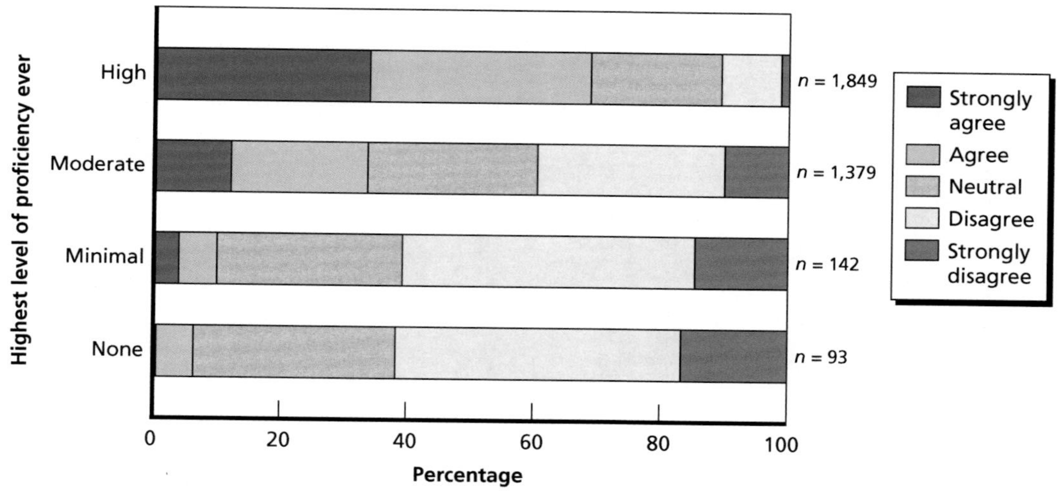

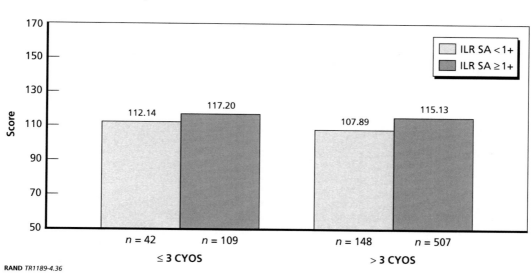

NOTE: Scores were averaged across three survey items: "I have always been good at learning languages,"
"I am good at learning new languages," and "Learning languages has always been a challenge for me."
RAND TR1189-4.35

Figure 4.36
Average DLAB Scores, by ILR Self-Assessment Score

RAND TR1189-4.36

- Are those who know second and third languages at a 1+ or higher more likely to know a fourth language than people with lower proficiency levels on the second and third languages?

Table 4.5 shows the weighted results addressing these questions. The first row in the table shows the proportion of all officers who know at least one language other than English. Unlike the first row, the populations for the second and third rows are restricted to only those who met the language requirement in the row above. So, in the first column, the proportion for the third language is out of those 94 percent of individuals who had a second language.

Figure 4.37
Average DLAB Scores, by Best-Ever Proficiency

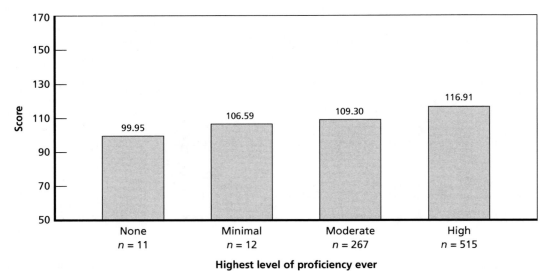

RAND TR1189-4.37

Table 4.5
Likelihood of Learning Additional Languages, by Proficiency in First Language

Analysis Set	Language Number	Reported Speaking Proficiency	Weighted Percentage	Number of Respondents Used for Calculating Percentages (unweighted)	
				Meeting the Requirement (numerator)	Total (denominator)
1	2nd	≥ 10 words	94	3,414	3,519
	3rd	≥ 10 words	69	2,524	3,414
	4th	≥ 10 words	48	1,402	2,524
2	2nd	≥ 1+[a]	45	2,364	3,519
	3rd	≥ 10 words[a]	76	1,849	2,364
	4th	≥ 10 words[a]	55	1,124	1,849
3	2nd	≥ 1+[a]	45	2,364	3,519
	3rd	≥ 1+[a]	29	697	2,364
	4th	≥ 10 words[a]	66	48	5,697

[a] ILR self-assessment scores.

Table 4.5 shows that the percentage of individuals who know at least ten words or more in a third language is slightly larger for the group that knows a second at 1+ or higher than for the group that knows at least ten words or more in a second (76 versus 69 percent). We can therefore conclude that it is more probable that an individual will know at least ten words or more in a third language if that individual knows a second at a 1+ or higher.

The results for knowing ten words or more in a fourth language, given that the second and third languages are at a level of 1+ or higher (66 percent), are significantly higher than when using the more relaxed criteria of ten words or more for the second or third languages

(48 and 55 percent, respectively). This tells us that, among these respondents, those who had at least elementary proficiency in a second language were more likely to have also learned a third language. And those who had at least elementary proficiency in a second and third language were more likely to have learned a fourth language. We also know from the studies described in Chapter Two that knowing a second language tends to facilitate the learning of a third and subsequent languages. Together, these findings suggest that a policy requiring working proficiency in a second language, if implemented successfully, could produce officers who are better prepared to learn additional languages.

Mandatory Proficiency Policies

In our survey, we presented statements about various types of language policies and asked officers to indicate their level of agreement with them. The results for those items are described below.

Relevance to Air Force Career and Mission Success

We asked respondents to react to the following three statements about the importance of language proficiency for career success:

- Foreign-language ability is not relevant to my job.
- Knowing a foreign language is important for my Air Force career.
- Knowing a foreign language won't help you get ahead in the Air Force.

We also asked about mission success:

- Foreign-language proficiency is an important warfighting skill.
- Foreign languages are irrelevant to mission success.

We then averaged the items to produce overall scores for career and mission success.[15] As can be seen in Figures 4.38 through 4.41, an overwhelming majority of officers agreed that language proficiency is important for mission success. In contrast, perceptions about language proficiency's relevance to career success were mixed, with only around 40 to 60 percent of officers agreeing that it is important for their own careers. This level of agreement about career success is a positive sign that many officers believe that language proficiency is important to them individually but also stresses that not all officers share that belief. These findings highlight an important discrepancy: that language is considered important to mission success but not as important for career success. This suggests that any language policy that would increase language requirements would need to be accompanied by organizational changes that would link language proficiency more directly to career success—for example, by including language skills in performance reviews and promotion decisions.

Mandatory Language Proficiency Policies

We asked respondents to rate the following two statements about mandatory language proficiency policies:

---

[15] Negatively worded items were reversed prior to averaging the responses.

Figure 4.38
Importance to Career Success, by ILR Self-Assessment Score

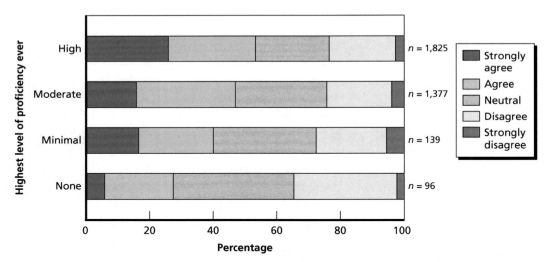

NOTE: Scores were averaged across "Foreign-language ability is not relevant to my job," "Knowing a foreign language is important for my Air Force career," and "Knowing a foreign language won't help you get ahead in the Air Force."
RAND *TR1189-4.38*

Figure 4.39
Importance to Career Success, by Best-Ever Proficiency

NOTE: Scores were averaged across "Foreign-language ability is not relevant to my job," "Knowing a foreign language is important for my Air Force career," and "Knowing a foreign language won't help you get ahead in the Air Force."
RAND *TR1189-4.39*

- All Air Force officers should be required to know a foreign language.
- It would be good if foreign-language proficiency (at a 2/2) were mandatory for promotion to Lt Col.

The results are shown in Figures 4.42 through 4.45. Overall, the response to the first item was mixed; nearly as many officers disagreed with as agreed with the statement. Attitudes about

**Figure 4.40
Importance to Mission Success, by ILR Self-Assessment Score**

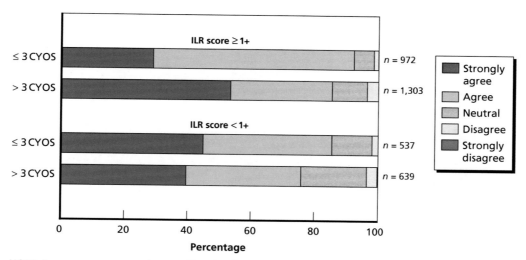

NOTE: Scores were averaged across "Foreign-language proficiency is an important warfighting skill" and "Foreign languages are irrelevant to mission success."
RAND TR1189-4.40

**Figure 4.41
Importance to Mission Success, by Best-Ever Proficiency**

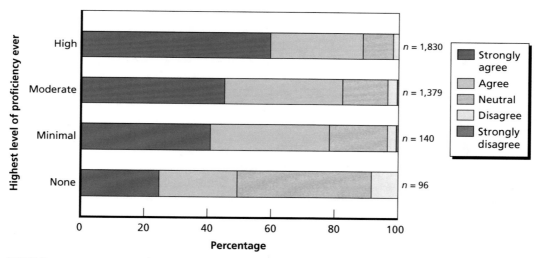

NOTE: Scores were averaged across "Foreign-language proficiency is an important warfighting skill" and "Foreign languages are irrelevant to mission success."
RAND TR1189-4.41

the second item were negative on average, with a majority of officers disagreeing with such a policy and more than one-quarter strongly disagreeing with it. This finding suggests that, at a minimum, such policies should be accompanied by a strong effort to engender buy-in from current officers. If not, such a policy is likely to be met with resistance from many throughout the officer ranks.

Figure 4.42
Views on Language Requirement for All, by ILR Self-Assessment Score

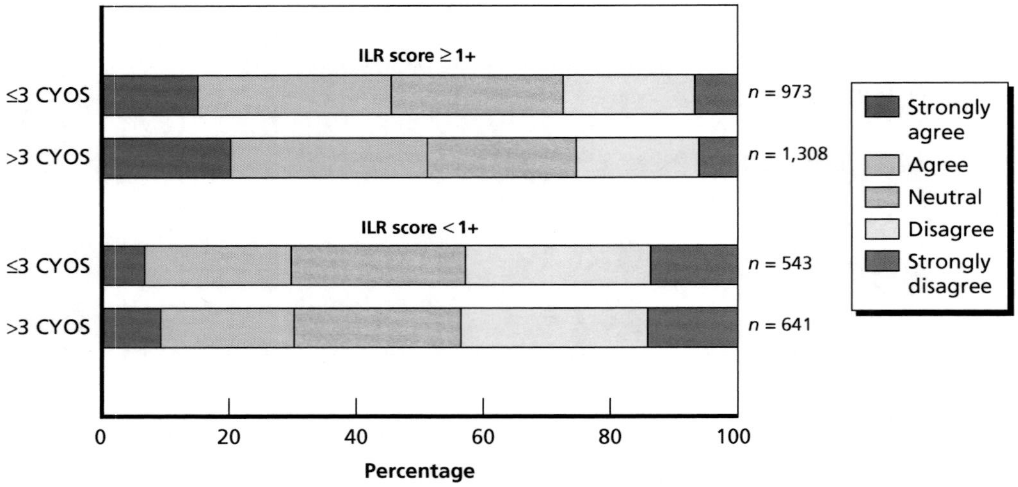

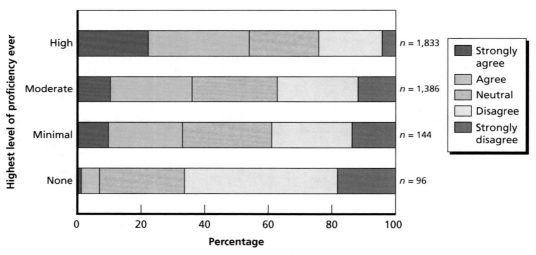

Survey item: "All Air Force officers should be required to know a foreign language."
RAND TR1189-4.42

Figure 4.43
Views on Language Requirement for All, by Best-Ever Proficiency

Survey item: "All Air Force officers should be required to know a foreign language."
RAND TR1189-4.43

Reflections on Learning a Language During College

We asked four questions about respondents' attitudes toward learning a language in college. These items were asked retrospectively of current Air Force officers and not of current college students; therefore, the results should be considered with caution. Nevertheless, we felt that asking current officers would at a minimum indicate how the current force views these issues. We asked them to think back to when they decided to join the Air Force, then asked whether they agreed or disagreed with the following:

Figure 4.44
Views on Language Requirement for Promotion to Lieutenant Colonel, by ILR Self-Assessment Score

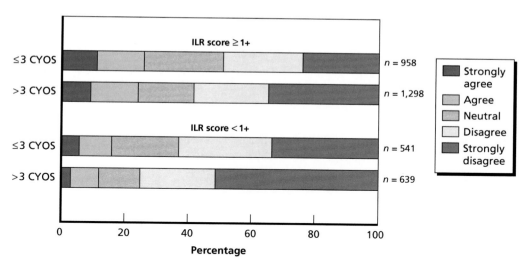

Survey item: "It would be good if foreign-language proficiency (at a 2/2) were mandatory for promotion to Lt Col."
RAND *TR1189-4.44*

Figure 4.45
Views on Language Requirement for Promotion to Lieutenant Colonel, by Best-Ever Proficiency

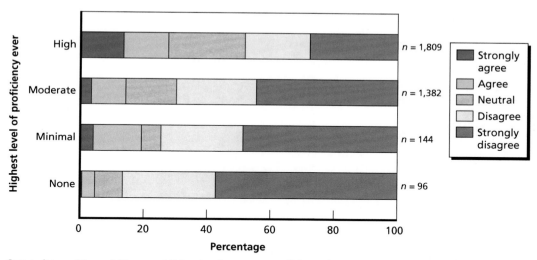

Survey item: "It would be good if foreign-language proficiency (at a 2/2) were mandatory for promotion to Lt Col."
RAND *TR1189-4.45*

- Learning a foreign language would have kept me from focusing on my major or other classes.
- I wish there had been more time for me to study a foreign language in college.
- I would have been willing to spend an extra year in college to learn a foreign language if the Air Force paid for it.

- I would have been willing to study a foreign language in college ONLY if it was Spanish, French, or German.

Figures 4.46 through 4.54 show the results by self-assessed language proficiency and CYOS.

According to Figures 4.46 and 4.47, a majority of officers with no proficiency believed that language courses would have prevented them from focusing on their major or other courses. Figure 4.48 shows that engineering majors were significantly more likely to view language courses as a distraction. Note that this finding is not necessarily inconsistent with the previous finding showing that engineering majors have levels of language skills similar to those of nonengineering majors (see Figure 4.11). Establishing a commissioning language-proficiency requirement was still perceived as more of a hindrance to engineering majors than to other types of majors.

The difference in perceptions between engineers and nonengineers is not surprising, given the highly structured sequencing in four-year course schedules for engineering majors. If the engineering course sequence is more demanding than those for other types of majors, engineering majors would need to work some sort of trade-off to meet the language requirement. Specifically, either performance in engineering courses would suffer, or it would take longer than is typical to complete the major. For the Air Force, one possible consequence of not expanding the time to complete the major despite adding a language proficiency requirement is that the pool of qualified officer candidates could come to include fewer engineers and/or engineers who are less successful in their majors.

Figures 4.49 through 4.52 show that, on average, officers both wished there had been time in college to study a language and would have been willing to spend an extra year doing just that if the Air Force had funded it. Because the comments were retrospective, it could be argued that such a sentiment reflects the attitude changes that may come with age, such as a desire to return to one's college days or developing an enhanced appreciation of learning.

Figure 4.46
Views on Language as Distraction from Other Curricula, by ILR Self-Assessment Score

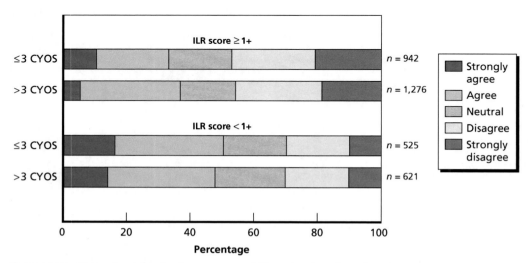

Survey item: "Learning a foreign language would have kept me from focusing on my major or other classes."

RAND TR1189-4.46

Figure 4.47
Views on Language as Distraction from Other Curricula, by Best-Ever Proficiency

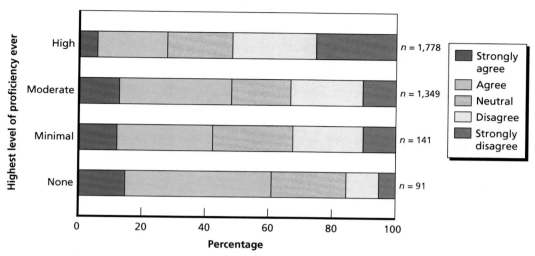

Survey item: "Learning a foreign language would have kept me from focusing on my major or other classes."
RAND TR1189-4.47

Figure 4.48
Views on Language as Distraction from Other Curricula, by Major, Engineering Versus Other

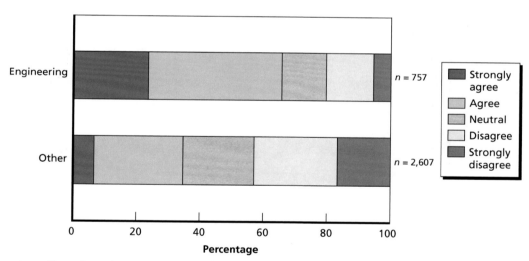

Survey item: "Learning a foreign language would have kept me from focusing on my major or other classes."
RAND TR1189-4.48

Although this argument is plausible, our data do not suggest that this is the case. Agreement did not differ meaningfully as CYOS increased, and as shown in Figure 4.49, even recent graduates felt positive about adding a year of college language study.

Despite the caveats and potential alternative explanations, this finding suggests that one solution to increasing officer language proficiency that few would find objectionable might be to offer an extra year's worth of full-time college tuition covering language courses, along with an expectation of a five-year rather than four-year degree.

Figure 4.49
Views on Additional College Time to Study Language, by ILR Self-Assessment Score

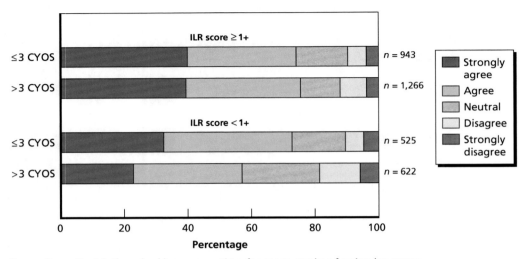

Survey item: "I wish there had been more time for me to study a foreign language in college."

RAND *TR1189-4.49*

Figure 4.50
Views on Additional College Time to Study Language, by Best-Ever Proficiency

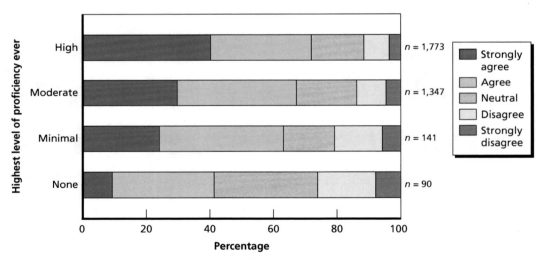

Survey item: "I wish there had been more time for me to study a foreign language in college."

RAND *TR1189-4.50*

Last, when asked if they would only be willing to study one of the most commonly taught languages (Spanish, German, or French), as shown in Figures 4.53 and 4.54, officers overwhelmingly responded "No." Fewer than 15 percent of recently commissioned officers agreed with the statement, and more 50 percent of all officers with no language proficiency disagreed. Coupled with the finding that the languages our respondents reported learning were

Figure 4.51
Views on Additional Air Force–Sponsored College Time to Study Language, by ILR Self-Assessment Score

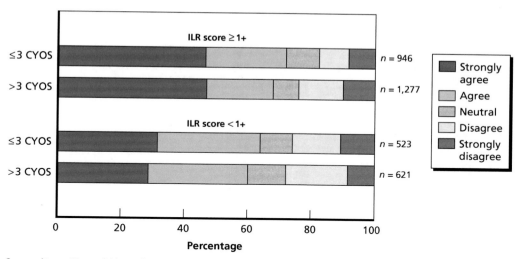

Survey item: "I would have been willing to spend an extra year in college to learn a foreign language if the Air Force paid for it."
RAND *TR1189-4.51*

Figure 4.52
Views on Additional Air Force–Sponsored College Time to Study Language, by Best-Ever Proficiency

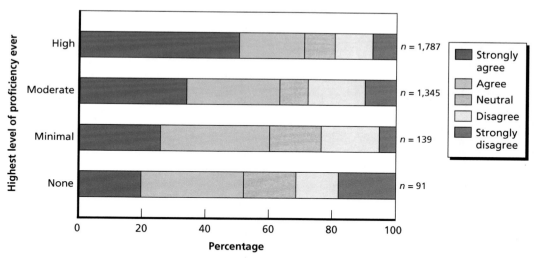

Survey item: "I would have been willing to spend an extra year in college to learn a foreign language if the Air Force paid for it."
RAND *TR1189-4.52*

overwhelmingly limited to these three, this suggests that no strong incentives exist for learning other types of languages and/or that learning opportunities in other languages are not readily available in many college settings.[16] This finding suggests offering much higher incentives to

---

[16] The latter is one finding from our review of ROTC detachments; see Appendix E.

Figure 4.53
Willingness to Study Languages Other Than Spanish, French, or German, by ILR Self-Assessment Score

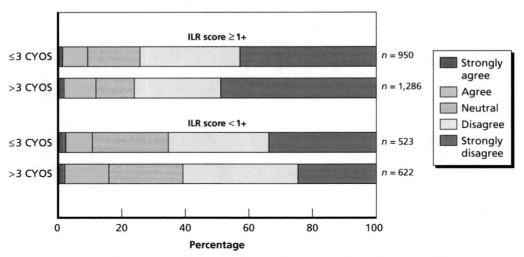

Survey item: "I would have been willing to study a foreign language in college ONLY if it was Spanish, French, or German."
RAND *TR1189-4.53*

Figure 4.54
Willingness to Study Languages Other than Spanish, French, or German, by Best-Ever Proficiency

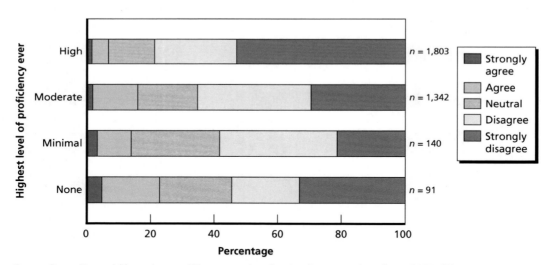

Survey item: "I would have been willing to study a foreign language in college ONLY if it was Spanish, French, or German."
RAND *TR1189-4.54*

students who study underrepresented languages and offering incentives to teachers and schools that provide courses in those languages.[17]

_____

[17] Note that the National Security Education Program (NSEP) does provide some opportunities along these lines. For more information, see the organization's website.

Language Requirement as Deterrent from Commissioning

In this section of the survey, we asked respondents to think back to when they joined the Air Force and respond to the following four statements assessing whether or not a language incentive would have deterred them from joining the Air Force:

- I would still have wanted to become an Air Force officer, even if there had been a foreign-language proficiency requirement.
- I would still have wanted to become an Air Force officer, even if it meant that I had to take foreign-language courses in college.
- I would have been discouraged from becoming an Air Force officer if I had to be proficient in a foreign language to qualify.
- If I had been required to study a foreign language to become an Air Force officer, I would have been less interested in joining the Air Force.

We averaged responses across the four items (see Figures 4.55 and 4.56).[18]

We also asked respondents to respond to statements about various college language opportunities and whether they would have made the respondents even more eager to join:

- Knowing the Air Force valued foreign-language proficiency would have made me even more interested in becoming an Air Force officer.

Figure 4.55
Language Is Not a Deterrent from Commissioning, by ILR Self-Assessment Score

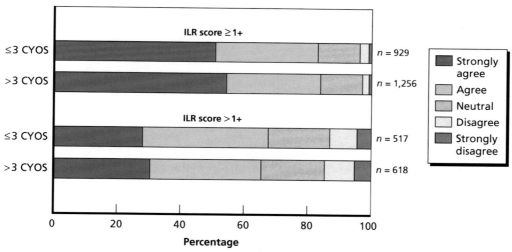

NOTE: Scores were averaged across "I would still have wanted to become an AF officer, even if there had been a foreign-language proficiency requirement," "I would still have wanted to become an AF officer, even if it meant that I had to take foreign-language courses in college," "I would have been discouraged from becoming an AF officer if I had to be proficient in a foreign language to qualify," "If I had been required to study a foreign language to become an AF officer, I would have been less interested in joining the AF."
RAND *TR1189-4.55*

---

[18] Negatively worded items were reversed prior to averaging the responses such that stronger agreement indicated a greater agreement that they would still have joined up.

Figure 4.56
Language Is Not a Deterrent from Commissioning, by Best-Ever Proficiency

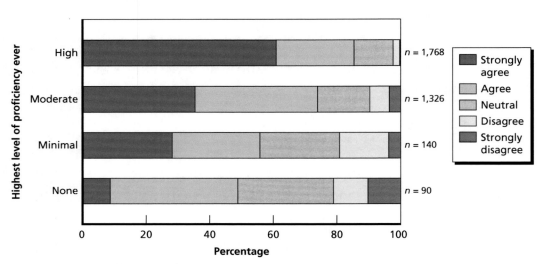

NOTE: Scores were averaged across four survey items: "I would still have wanted to become an AF officer, even if there had been a foreign-language proficiency requirement," "I would still have wanted to become an AF officer, even if it meant that I had to take foreign-language courses in college," "I would have been discouraged from becoming an AF officer if I had to be proficient in a foreign language to qualify," "If I had been required to study a foreign language to become an AF officer, I would have been less interested in joining the AF."
RAND *TR1189-4.56*

- If the Air Force had provided an incentive for learning a foreign language while I was in college (such as extra pay), I would have been even more interested in becoming an Air Force officer.
- If the Air Force had provided an opportunity for learning a foreign language while I was in college (such as a summer abroad program), I would have been even more interested in becoming an Air Force officer.

Results for each item are presented individually in Figures 4.57 through 4.62. None of the results from Figures 4.57 through 4.62 showed meaningful differences by CYOS; however, in all of the figures, the level of agreement is consistently and significantly related to ILR self-assessment speaking scores and highest level of self-reported language proficiency. Specifically, an overwhelming majority of those with higher self-reported proficiency tended to believe that various language-learning opportunities would have made them even more willing to join the Air Force and that they would not have been deterred by a language requirement; only about half of those with no language proficiency reported similar agreement about being deterred, and far fewer agreed that the various language opportunities would have positively affected their interest in becoming Air Force officers.

These results suggest that various language incentives in college would be most attractive to those who already had some language skills or those who were likely to obtain at least some proficiency in a language in the future. Our findings also suggest that a language proficiency requirement might not deter a majority of potential officers from joining. Nevertheless, not all officers shared that sentiment. Our survey findings indicate that, for as many as 20 percent of officers with minimal to no language proficiency (see Figure 4.56), the existence of such a requirement might have dissuaded them from joining the Air Force.

Figure 4.57
Interest in Air Force if It Provided a College Opportunity for Language Learning, by ILR Self-Assessment Score

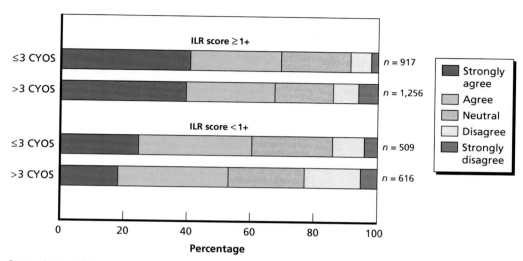

Survey item: "If the AF had provided an opportunity for learning a foreign language while I was in college (such as a summer abroad program), I would have been even more interested in becoming an AF officer."
RAND TR1189-4.57

Figure 4.58
Interest in Air Force if It Provided a College Opportunity for Language Learning, by Best-Ever Proficiency

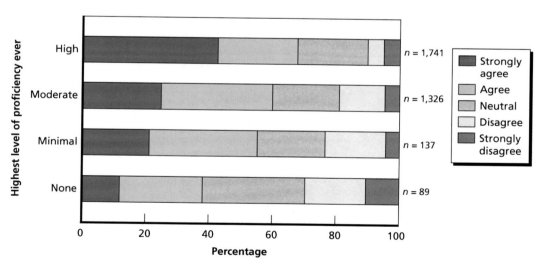

Survey item: "If the AF had provided an opportunity for learning a foreign language while I was in college (such as a summer abroad program), I would have been even more interested in becoming an AF officer."
RAND TR1189-4.58

Figure 4.63 summarizes all the attitudinal and opinion items on the survey. It compares the levels of agreement on the various retrospective items to the levels of agreement on the self-efficacy scale, the mission and career success scales, and the language policy items. For simplicity, only the results for recently commissioned officers (less than three CYOS) are shown. The

Figure 4.59
Interest in Air Force if It Provided Incentives for Language Learning, by ILR Self-Assessment Score

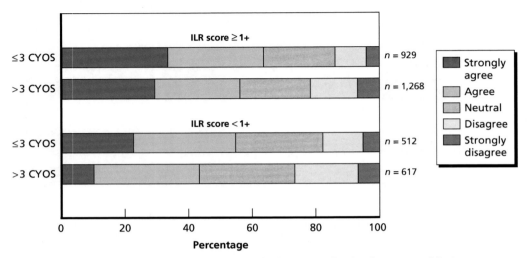

Survey item: "If the AF had provided an incentive for learning a foreign language while I was in college (such as extra pay), I would have been even more interested in becoming an AF officer."
RAND TR1189-4.59

Figure 4.60
Interest in Air Force if It Provided Incentives for Language Learning, by Best-Ever Proficiency

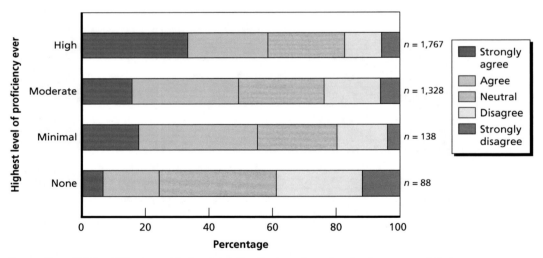

Survey item: "If the AF had provided an incentive for learning a foreign language while I was in college (such as extra pay), I would have been even more interested in becoming an AF officer."
RAND TR1189-4.60

importance of language to mission success received the strongest agreement among all items and scales, followed closely by indications that a language requirement would not be a deterrent to joining. The level of agreement for relevance for personal career success was noticeably lower than the levels for more than one-half the items and scales. Policies requiring second-language proficiency were among the items with which officers most disagreed. This figure

Figure 4.61
Interest in Air Force if It Valued Language, by ILR Self-Assessment Score

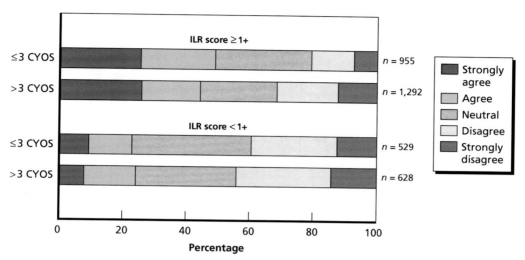

Survey item: "Knowing the Air Force valued foreign-language proficiency would have
made me even more interested in becoming an AF officer."
RAND TR1189-4.61

Figure 4.62
Interest in Air Force if It Valued Language, by Best-Ever Proficiency

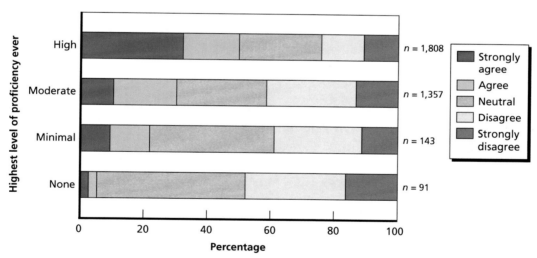

Survey item: "Knowing the Air Force valued foreign-language proficiency would have made
me even more interested in becoming an AF officer."
RAND TR1189-4.62

also shows that, although there are clear differences in agreement by language proficiency,
the relative agreement across items is similar. For example, the paid college language-learning
opportunities, such as getting to spend an extra year in college or studying abroad, were viewed
positively even among lower-proficiency officers.

Taken together, these results are promising because they reveal that the clear majority of
officers

Figure 4.63
Strength of Agreement on All Attitude Scales and Items for Officers with Fewer Than Three CYOS

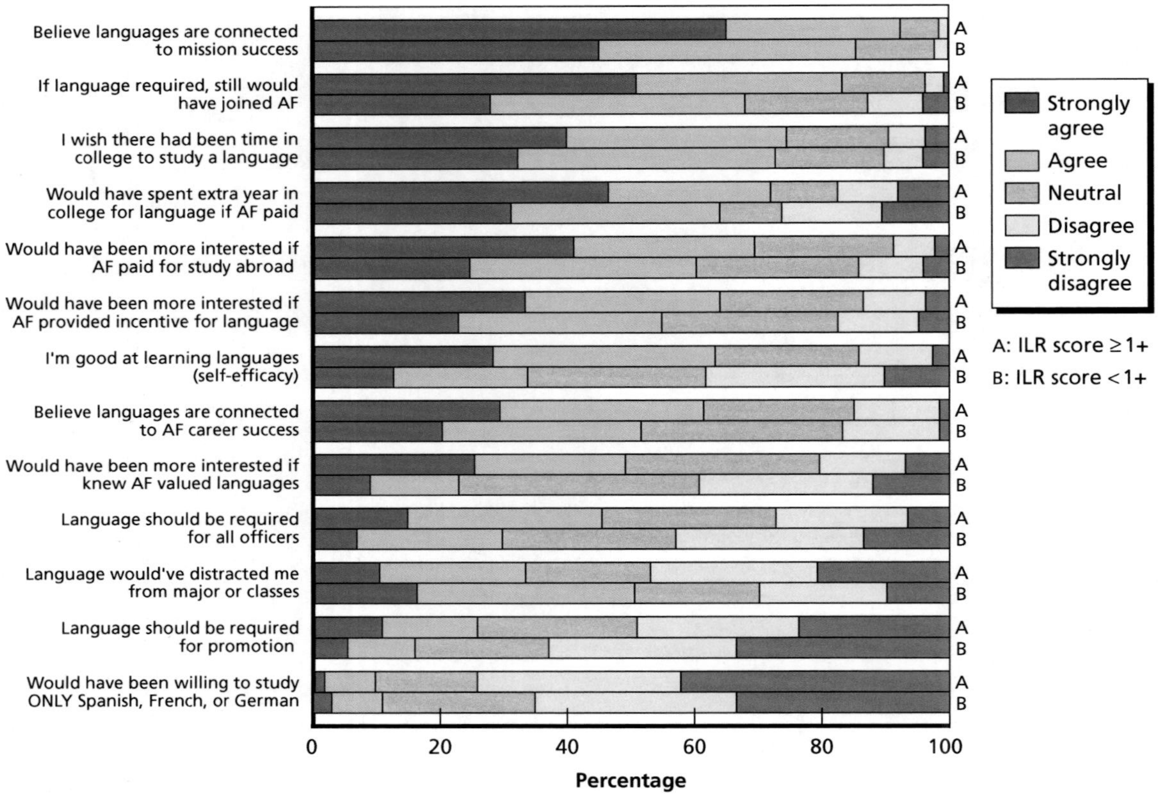

NOTE: Results are ordered by level of agreement among those with ILR self-assessment scores ≥1+.
RAND TR1189-4.63

- believed that language is important for mission success
- would not have been deterred from joining the Air Force by a language requirement
- wished there had been more time to study a language and would have been willing to spend an extra year in college to learn a language if the Air Force funded it
- would have been even more interested in the Air Force if it provided incentives for learning a language and/or paid for study abroad
- would have been willing to learn languages other than those most commonly taught.

These findings suggest opportunities for future policies to encourage more officer candidates to gain language proficiency through additional study and to learn less commonly taught languages that are of greater strategic value.

Incentives and Disincentives for Learning a Second Language

As mentioned previously, one purpose of establishing a new language policy would be to motivate officers or officer candidates to improve their language skills. We therefore asked respondents to indicate which incentives for and concerns about learning a language would affect their willingness to learn a new language. Tables 4.6 and 4.7 show the average ratings (ranging from 7 = strongly agree to 1 = strongly disagree) on each incentive and concern by proficiency levels.

The results show that certain incentives consistently outrank others, regardless of best-ever proficiency. Top ranked incentives were:

- having the Air Force pay for the language training
- getting to take the language training during regular work hours
- taking classes with a spouse
- getting to attend an immersion program in a foreign country.

The lowest ranked incentive was taking language classes after regular work hours.

There were clear differences by language proficiency in the overall level of agreement across all items. Specifically, the higher the language proficiency, the higher the average level of agreement. For example, those with no language proficiency slightly disagreed that mandatory language proficiency for promotion to lieutenant colonel would be an incentive, while those with minimal or higher proficiency slightly agreed with this incentive.

There were other subtle differences in the rank ordering of the incentives depending on language skill. For example, for those reporting high (6 or higher) or moderate (3 to 5) proficiency, being assigned to a desirable foreign location was the fourth highest incentive; however, for the low and moderate proficiency groups, that item ranked much lower.

Similar differences can be seen in the ratings of concerns (Table 4.7). Spending personal time and being passed over for promotion because officers are not focusing on their primary job duties topped the list, and those with no language proficiency agreed that they would be better off doing something that supports the mission. This again indicates that, for some, the connection between language skills and mission success is unclear. The item that officers saw as least concerning was the possibility of being seen as un-American or unpatriotic. The statements in the list that officers did not disagree with should certainly be considered in deciding how to institute an effective policy.

In addition to asking respondents to react to our list of potential incentives and disincentives, we also included an open-ended text box where respondents could add other answers. More than 400 officers provided write-in responses in the incentives section; more than 200 respondents did so in the concerns section. Among the write-in comments, the three most common incentives were

- opportunities to use language skills
- preferred duty assignments, locations, and deployments
- opportunities for immersion experiences, exchange programs, short-term temporary duty assignments, and other travel experiences.

The most common write-in concerns were that

- it would strain limited resources, both those of the Air Force and of individuals, given their existing time and work demands
- the Air Force does not value language capabilities
- knowing languages is a necessity for only a few career fields.

Table 4.6
Level of Agreement with Incentives by Best-Ever Proficiency

Item Stem: I would be more likely to invest effort in learning another language if:	No Language at All (mean)	Proficiency (mean)		
		Minimal (0–2)	Moderate (3–5)	High (6–8)
The AF would pay for my language training	5.3	5.8	6.1	6.4
I could do the language training during my regular work hours	5.1	5.7	5.7	6.0
I could take language classes with my spouse	5.0	5.1	5.2	5.5
I could attend an immersion program in a foreign country	5.0	5.2	5.7	6.1
I would be learning a language that is useful in the private sector	4.6	5.2	5.1	5.2
I would get extra pay while receiving language training	4.5	4.8	5.1	5.4
I would get extra pay for knowing another language	4.2	4.5	4.8	5.1
I could take language classes with my friends or coworkers	4.2	4.6	4.7	5.0
Knowing the language meant that I would be assigned to a desirable foreign location	4.1	4.8	5.4	5.8
I could learn it by myself on my own time at my own pace	4.1	3.9	4.4	4.7
Knowing the language would make me more respected by AF leadership and/or peers	3.8	4.5	4.6	5.0
By knowing the language, I would be viewed more favorably in the AF promotion process	3.6	4.7	4.6	5.1
Foreign-language proficiency was mandatory for promotion to Lt Col	3.1	4.6	4.5	4.9
I could do the language training after my regular work hours so that it wouldn't interfere with my normal AF duties	3.1	3.4	3.8	4.0

NOTE: Sample sizes ranged from 83 to 93 in the no language group; 133 to 143 in the minimal proficiency group; 1,242 to 1,371 in the moderate proficiency group; and 1,669 to 1,839 in the high proficiency group.

Key:
Level of Disagreement

Strong (1.0–2.0)	Moderate (2.1–3.0)	Slight (3.1–3.5)

Level of Agreement

Neutral (3.6–4.4)	Slight (4.5–4.9)	Moderate (5.0–5.9)	Strong (6.0–7.0)

Table 4.7
Level of Agreement with Concerns by Best-Ever Proficiency

Item Stem: I would be concerned about learning another language because I think I might be:	No Language at All (mean)	Proficiency (mean)		
		Minimal (0–2)	Moderate (3–5)	High (6–8)
Expected to do the training during my personal time	5.2	5.0	4.9	4.5
Passed over for promotion if I don't focus on my current duties and other professional development opportunities	4.9	4.5	4.5	4.4
Better off doing other work that supports the mission	4.6	4.2	4.3	3.7
Required to spend time away from my family during the training	4.5	4.7	4.3	4.0
Stovepiped into a certain type of career	4.5	4.0	4.1	3.9
Not good at learning languages	4.5	4.4	3.6	2.4
More likely to be deployed outside the US	4.2	4.2	3.9	3.5
More likely to be deployed to a combat zone	4.2	4.0	3.8	3.5
More likely to be sent outside the wire	4.2	3.9	3.8	3.4
Required to spend time away from my regular work duties during the training	4.2	4.0	3.9	3.3
Likely to fail the tests	3.5	3.2	2.8	2.0
Acquiring a useless skill	3.4	2.5	2.4	1.9
Likely to embarrass myself	2.9	3.1	2.8	2.0
Thought of as unpatriotic or un-American	2.3	1.7	1.7	1.5

NOTE: Sample sizes range from 88 to 92 in the no language group; 139 to 144 in the minimal proficiency group; 1,329 to 1,360 in the moderate proficiency group; and 1,776 to 1,819 in the high proficiency group.

Key:

Level of Disagreement

Strong (1.0–2.0)	Moderate (2.1–3.0)	Slight (3.1–3.5)

Level of Agreement

Neutral (3.6–4.4)	Slight (4.5–4.9)	Moderate (5.0–5.9)	Strong (6.0–7.0)

Overall, the write-in responses, along with the results in Tables 4.6 and 4.7, suggest that promising ways to increase language proficiency would include

- paying for language training and materials
- making training available during work hours and providing time to attend
- offering classes with spouses
- offering immersion experiences and time to participate.

Promising ways to eliminate perceived obstacles to language learning would include

- providing opportunities during work hours for learning and maintenance
- factoring efforts to improve and maintain skills into promotion decisions.

These perceived incentives and disincentives suggest directions for policies that would motivate officers to learn languages and reduce barriers to participation and buy-in.

Open-Ended Responses

At 11 different points throughout the main portion of the survey, we included text boxes in which respondents could respond to open-ended questions.[19] Out of the 3,519 completed surveys, 38.9 percent of the respondents offered a comment on one or more of these questions.[20]

Ten of the write-in opportunities appeared in response to checking "other (please specify)." For example, in the section examining language-learning incentives, we presented the statement, "I would be more likely to invest effort in learning another language if," followed by a list of factors that we thought might be highly motivating. Knowing that we could not foresee all potential incentives respondents might see, we included a 14th item, "I would receive other benefits, advantages, or rewards, such as (please specify)."[21]

In addition to the "other (please specify)" options throughout the survey, we invited respondents at the very end to write-in any additional comments they might have about learning languages (what we refer to here as the "additional comments" item). On this question, nearly one-third of people completing the survey (a total of 1,151 responses) had something to offer, frequently at length.

To summarize the comments, we coded responses for each of the 11 open-ended text boxes in the survey. We started with an initial set of categories that reflected the most common and the most pertinent themes or ideas among the responses. Once we had a comprehensive list of idea categories, a researcher reviewed each comment and checked off every idea it mentioned. In our coding process, a particular category could only be counted once for each respondent's comment; however, a single comment could be coded as mentioning multiple categories. In this way, we were able to determine the total number of people who mentioned a particular category for each open-ended response on the survey. A second researcher repeated

---

[19] Note that the demographic section included additional write-in boxes.

[20] The 38.9 percent reported here is unweighted. The weighted percent, interpreted as the estimated percentage of officers who would have provided a comment if our respondents had been a simple random sample of officers, is 33.4 percent.

[21] Note that the results for this particular write-in item were discussed in the previous section.

the coding process on a sample of items, which we then checked against the first researcher's coding to ensure that the coding process was working properly.

The overall results for the "other (please specify)" items and the "additional comments" item are discussed separately below.

"Other (Please Specify)" Items

Table 4.8 briefly summarizes the most common responses to the "other (please specify)" options throughout the survey. Appendix F contains results for each item in much greater detail, including definitions and examples and the number of people expressing each theme.

Taken together, these responses suggest that many Air Force officers are amenable to the idea of developing language capabilities. This view is, however, tempered by the uncertainty of meeting additional demands with existing support, high operational tempo, and little or no time to for developing such skills. Other common concerns were that a language would be difficult to acquire in some career fields and that the Air Force would not utilize the skill. This suggests some level of skepticism within the officer corps about the lasting effects of these policies or about senior institutional commitment to seeing them through. A variety of approaches to gaining proficiency were mentioned, but a common theme is that immersion is especially valuable.

"Additional Comments" Item

About half of our respondents (53.4 percent) provided comments here.[22] Because there was no specific question to guide responses, the overall content was quite diverse. For this reason, we grouped the results according to four broad themes. As shown in Table 4.9, the most frequent theme by far was potential barriers. For more-detailed information about the frequency and variety of comments for each of the themes, see Appendix F.

---

[22] The weighted percentage is 48.6 percent.

Table 4.8
Most Common "Other (Please Specify)" Write-In Responses

Write-In Opportunities			
Survey Question	Total Responses[a]	Most Common Themes	Other Recurring Themes
Incentives: Other benefits, advantages, and rewards associated with learning languages	406	Opportunity to use skills Preferred duty assignments, locations, and deployments	Immersion experiences through exchange programs, short-term TDYs, or other travel opportunities.
Disincentives: Other concerns associated with learning languages	197	Strain on limited resources, including time and work demands	Air Force doesn't value foreign-language capabilities Language capability is unnecessary for all career fields
Where did you learn the language?	448	Immersion experience through travel or living in-residence	Self-study activities using software programs, DVDs, or study manuals Exposure in community or through job Church or missionary training
Why did you take this language in college?	297	Satisfy a degree or scholarship requirement	Planned to travel or live abroad Personal development to improve language skills
Why did you take this language in high school?	74	Prerequisite for college or to be competitive for a program	Requirement for graduation Personal development to maintain or develop language skills
What other language-related courses did you take in college?	206	Language focused such as phonetics, linguistics, and grammar World affairs such as political science, government, and history	Immersion courses in a study abroad program
How have you maintained your language skills since college or high school?		Traveling, living abroad, and various TDYs Reading books, newspapers, and the web	Reading books, newspapers, and the web Regular communication with others in family or in community
College	290		
High school	71		

Table 4.8—Continued

Write-In Opportunities

Survey Question	Total Responses[a]	Most Common Themes	Other Recurring Themes
What other DLI training have you received?	76	As part of another formal training course such as Air Advisors Academy Language training provided by DLI instructors Self-guided using activities provided by DLI	Attended specific language-based training program such as AFPAK [AFPAK Hands program]
What other language-related military training have you received?	52	As part of formal education, such as the U.S. Marine Corps Command and Staff College Immersion program or experience	Training prior to deployment Provided by tutor or in a one-on-one environment
What other language-related nonmilitary training have you received?	15	Church or missionary training	N/A

[a] Indicates the total number of write-ins on this survey question.

Table 4.9
Broad Themes and Most Common "Additional Comments" Write-In Responses

Write-In Themes			
Broad Theme	**Mentions**	**Most Common Idea in the Theme**	**Other Frequent Ideas**
Positive comments	418	General support for language development or willingness to learn	Language skills benefit the mission, facilitate job duties, or help build stronger relations with other countries
Potential barriers	979	Having sufficient time to learn and maintain while balancing job duties or personal obligations Concern that languages would not be fully utilized by the Air Force	Concern that the Air Force is not fully supportive or does not fully promote foreign-language capabilities
Implementation	441	Emphasized the importance of immersion for development and retention of language skills	Air Force should limit support of language to specific career fields, languages, or missions Air Force should provide duty time to learn and retain language skills
Resources	465	Indicated desire to have access to programs and resources for developing and maintaining language skills	Positive and negative comments regarding Rosetta Stone and DLI

CHAPTER FIVE

Conclusions and Recommendations

Conclusions

The first of our two broad research questions addressed whether it was feasible to require officer candidates to achieve a minimum score of 2/2 or 3/3 on a language proficiency exam. The short answer is no, at least for the near term. Our survey results suggested that very few officer applicants would meet the proposed levels of proficiency simply through college courses. Indeed, the amount of coursework required to meet such levels of proficiency (five semesters being an absolute minimum for category I languages) is likely to far exceed what could fit into a standard college curriculum. Most officers in our survey reported having taken between zero and two semesters of language in college. Given this finding, taking a minimum of five semesters would have meant eliminating other courses or imposing a course load heavier than that required for graduation. Moreover, knowing that some who had actually majored or minored in a language or had majored in foreign-area studies reported scores below 2/2; it seems unlikely that five semesters would produce a 2/2 level for those who had not.

Our second broad research question addressed the potential consequences of implementing a language proficiency requirement for officers, and the answer is complex. First, such a requirement could affect the characteristics of the officer force in many ways, some positive and some negative. Since about one-half of recently commissioned officers reported language skills below 1+, requiring all officers to enter at a 2/2 would distinctly improve overall skills. However, the types of languages spoken, the extent to which they are maintained, and the extent to which the Air Force utilizes the skills all factor into how beneficial this change would be on a practical level.

Second, not all will be able or willing to meet this requirement—even if offered training—so the pool of eligible officers would certainly be smaller. This could affect several other aspects of the officer force. For example, the personality, technical background, and demographics of commissioned officers may change. To the extent that language learning is related to certain personality traits, selecting only people who are proficient at a 2/2 or higher could yield a group of officers with more homogeneous personalities, which could in turn affect other aspects of workplace performance.[1] In addition, engineering majors are one-half as likely to be required to study languages as other majors (only about 20 to 25 percent of engineers reported such a requirement), and a five-semester requirement would thus affect engineers more than other majors. Moreover, such a change would likely force engineers either to take longer to

---

[1]   Given that personality is related to other workplace outcomes, including apparently unrelated aspects of job performance, the relationships between language proficiency and personality need to be better understood to keep a foreign-language proficiency policy from having unintended detrimental effects on other important workplace outcomes.

complete their degree or to carry a heavier course load (which could diminish the engineering skills they could be expected to have on entering the Air Force).

Current demographics suggest that the officer candidates most likely to attain a 2/2 or 3/3 level in a second language are either heritage speakers, nonheritage speakers who are exposed to extensive language curricula in elementary and secondary schools, or those who majored in a language in college.[2] None of these are in large supply. Heritage speakers constitute less than 20 percent of the U.S. population (Shin and Bruno, 2003). Only a small proportion of U.S. elementary and secondary schools offer foreign-language instruction. And the population of language majors (especially in languages useful for national security) is limited.

Furthermore, elementary and secondary school language instruction is more likely to be available in urban locales and areas with higher socioeconomic status, and the amount of language study undertaken differs by race (see Rhodes and Pufahl, 2009; KewalRamani et al., 2007, Figure 12d; and U.S. Department of Education, 2005, Table 25-3). Changes that affect who is likely to qualify for commissioning could have implications for diversity in the Air Force if none of those conditions changes. Thus, even though some speakers might be more likely than others to attain a 2/2 or 3/3 in a language other than English, none of these groups would provide enough qualified individuals to fulfill the Air Force's personnel needs. Note that efforts to target recruiting toward any one of these groups would be unwise because the likely result would be further unintended changes to demographics and diversity in the officer corps.

Third, dissatisfaction with the policy among candidates and current officers could lead to turnover and reduced organizational commitment. We know from the literature and our survey findings that motivation and attitudes toward language learning affect outcomes. Our survey showed that attitudes toward the mandatory policies were not overwhelmingly positive, and in some cases, the policies might have discouraged individuals from joining the Air Force in the first place. Tying language proficiency to other career milestones could be motivational for those who already possess language skills but could deter some from joining the Air Force who do not already possess such skills and would be forced to acquire them.

Finally, research on language attrition (see Chapter Two) and the substantial differences we found between highest proficiency ever and current proficiency highlight the tendency for proficiency to diminish without maintenance. Therefore, as a consequence of instituting a 2/2 requirement, the Air Force would need to devote resources to maintaining the language skills of those who do not regularly use them at work or socially.

Recommendations

Our survey and review of the literature have yielded a number of key insights and suggested recommendations for building a language-enabled officer force. We explain these in the sec-

---

[2]   While heritage speakers as a group might appear to be a promising source of second-language proficient individuals, we caution against making them a primary source for the Air Force's need for language skills. First, their levels of proficiency vary significantly, and many may still need extensive additional training for their skills to be of use in a military context (Bermel and Kagan, 2000; Kagan and Dillon, 2008). Second, many heritage language speakers in the United States speak Spanish, a language of low priority for national security. Third, focusing exclusively on this small population as the solution to meeting language proficiency requirements would overlook the potential of many other equally capable non–heritage speakers and may have the unintended consequence of disenfranchising these other language learners from the organization or discouraging their pursuit of increased proficiency.

tions that follow. We also identify the key potential consequences of our recommendations that policymakers should consider.[3]

Tailor Policies to Desired Outcomes, Including Different Policies for Different Outcomes

In our project planning meetings, Air Force leaders mentioned a number of reasons for the Air Force to develop the language skills of officers and airmen. These reasons included such worthwhile goals as improving their awareness of other cultures, their ability to interact in culturally appropriate ways, the speed with which they could learn new languages, and their ability to communicate in host nations.

These goals for language policy are very different from one another, and requiring all officers to have a second language is unlikely to be an effective or efficient way to meet them all. Furthermore, these forcewide goals are distinct from the need to produce professionals for specific language-intensive career fields. Given that different policies would be needed for each goal, we urge policymakers to keep them distinct.

Each of the following five goals for a second-language requirement was raised in our meetings with Air Force leaders and would best be fulfilled with its own tailored policy:

1. **Develop and maintain language professionals for specific career fields.** Much of existing Air Force language policy aims at developing personnel in specific language-intensive career fields, such as regional affairs specialists, public affairs specialists, and cryptologic linguists. While it was not the focus of this report, this vital component of Air Force language policy confuses discussion of other, forcewide, efforts.[4]

   Part of the confusion is due to a misconception that a new policy designed to develop a language-enabled Air Force in general would replace existing efforts to develop personnel for specific language-professional career fields. However, development of these "foreign-language professionals" should be driven by and tailored to the unique needs of the career fields in question. Language professionals are a highly select group of individuals chosen for their high language-learning potential who undergo lengthy, highly intensive, and structured DoD-controlled training. Such training would likely be infeasible or inappropriate for the rest of the Air Force. The typical Air Force officer has neither the time nor the resources for such an intensive program, and it would be impractical for the Air Force to channel the necessary resources to intensively train all officers. Given that the general population's training would inevitably be spread out over the course of their careers and far less rigorous, it is likely that curriculum requirements would differ. The language proficiency outcomes that foreign-language professionals' training environments produce are thus also likely to be much higher than those achievable in the general Air Force population with an equivalent amount of training.

---

[3] Many aspects of our recommendations are similar to those in a number of existing documents and articles providing guidance on language policy (for examples, see DoD, 2007b; DoD, 2005; Chairman of the Joint Chiefs of Staff, 2010; House Armed Services Committee, 2008; Conway, 2005; Conway, 2010). This study's findings provide empirical support for many of the practices they suggest.

[4] Efforts to develop language professionals are one of several goals discussed in official statements regarding language development. See, for example, DoD, 2005.

2. **Have a variety of officers in all types of jobs who can speak to and understand host nationals in their native languages.** Fulfilling this goal means developing language-enabled officers who speak the languages of the countries to which they are deployed and can communicate effectively with host nationals, third-country nationals, or coalition partners in their native languages.[5] Knowing a local language is critical for speaking with or listening to host nationals and for reading in a host-nation's language. Officers may also need to communicate with third-country nationals speaking yet another language. These situations highlight the need for Air Force officers who know the languages that most support U.S. national security. Spanish, French, and German, the most commonly taught languages, are of little use in many deployments.

   Any new officer accession language policy must thus address the scarcity of skills in strategically important languages. One way to do this is to make language proficiency a key consideration in deployment assignments. The second way is to build capacity in languages that are not sufficiently represented. For deployments, it is vital for commanders to know who they can call on for the host country language or for the languages of third country nationals and coalition partners.

   The Air Force has a long road ahead to build capacity in a variety of languages. Our survey found that many languages of current strategic importance are sorely underrepresented, even at low levels of proficiency. This suggests that the more underrepresented, difficult, and strategically important the language, the greater the reward should be for learning it and using it on the job. This also suggests that the existing Foreign Language Proficiency Bonus is not an adequate incentive for learning underrepresented languages. Possible changes to this bonus are discussed in depth below.

3. **Have a variety of culturally competent personnel in all types of jobs to interact with host nationals.** Cultural competence enables an individual to behave appropriately within a culture's social norms, even when relying on an interpreter to communicate.[6] Linguistic competence, in contrast, enables the person to communicate with the speakers of a given language in a common tongue. While these two competencies are clearly complementary, they are distinct: Possessing one does not imply possessing the other. Given that cultural competence is an important Air Force development goal, cultural training for that specific purpose should continue rather than give way to the perhaps less effective and certainly less efficient avenue of language training.

   That is not to say that language proficiency should not be pursued for other reasons or that cultural skills could not be part of language training. Both cultural skills and language skills are valuable, and policies to build cultural competence could strengthen efforts to develop high levels of proficiency in a given language. Therefore, the policies for linguistic competence and cultural competence should be complementary, but distinct, and should acknowledge that each addresses a separate skill set.

---

[5] This is one of the explicitly stated goals in many force development initiatives. See, for example, Chairman of the Joint Chiefs of Staff, 2010.

[6] As an example, according to DoD, 2005, The Strategic Planning Guidance (SPG) for fiscal years 2006–2011 listed creating foundational language and cultural expertise among the goals for language transformation. In addition, language development is often pointed to in statements urging development of more cross-cultural skills. See, for example, the DoD June 2007 Summit's section titled "Action: Build A DoD Regional and Cultural Capabilities Strategic Plan" (DoD, 2007b), which describes language, regional, and cultural skills as being part of the strategic plan to build regional and cultural capabilities.

4. **Make all personnel more culturally sensitive and aware.** Cultural sensitivity and awareness are broader and more general attributes than the cultural competence we described above, even though they are related concepts. A person does not automatically acquire cultural awareness, sensitivity, or understanding through the study of languages. Cultural sensitivity may result from other individual characteristics or experiences, such as interaction with people from other cultures and an innate ability to empathize. It does not necessarily result from learning another language, especially if language learning occurs in a classroom, without interaction with the corresponding culture. Again, training and education specifically focused on interaction with individuals from other cultures, generating empathy, and increasing awareness of what life is like in various places in the world would be far less costly and more effective than language training to address this goal.

5. **Have personnel in all jobs who can learn other languages more easily and quickly.** Some Air Force leaders also cited having a "language-primed" force, one whose officers are able to learn subsequent languages more easily than a second language, as another desirable outcome of a language proficiency requirement. Past research has found that knowing a second language can improve one's ability to learn a third language, especially when the languages are similar. However, a completely language-primed force— in which all officers possessed at least limited working proficiency in a second language—might mean a substantial reduction in the qualified candidate pool. Moreover, there is no guarantee that someone who knows a second language could learn a new language in just-in-time training and achieve even modest levels of skill, even if the language is similar. Learning the more difficult category IV languages will still require intensive training.

   Language aptitude, which includes a range of individual characteristics, is likely to be a better, more practical predictor of language-learning success than priming through second-language learning.[7] The resource demands of such training suggest that it is more feasible to select, train, and offer maintenance activities to a subset of officers in key languages than it is to do so for all officers, especially given that not all will end up using the languages in their jobs. Our findings on the survey also demonstrate that simply knowing a second language does not make one *much* more likely to fulfill the potential to actually learn a third or fourth, even if there is an increased capability to do so.

   It would thus be impractical to suggest preparing for the language needs of the future, which are largely unknown, by allowing students to study any language of their choosing. Those who have studied one of most commonly taught languages—Spanish, French, or German—find little opportunity to use it on the job. These languages offer few linguistic transfer advantages to those trying to learn such languages as Arabic and Chinese.

   We cannot emphasize strongly enough that developing language proficiency and creating language-enabled officers would take extensive amounts of time and resources, even with language-primed officers. Just-in-time language training is an effective way to teach individuals a selection of survival phrases and should continue for all personnel

---

[7] We were not, however, able to test that relationship in this study.

prior to deployment. However, such training should not lead anyone to be thought of as "language enabled." Instead, this term should be used only for those who are making a continuous and concerted effort to develop meaningful and measurable skills in one or more languages other than English.

With this in mind, we recommend setting aside the goal of creating a language-primed force of individuals who can quickly learn another language when the need arises. Instead, we recommend focusing on the long-term development of proficiency among a subset of officers in a wide variety of languages so officers who are proficient in a given language will be available when the need arises. Specifically, the Air Force could ensure that large groups of personnel of varying levels of proficiency are available for each strategic language and that small groups of individuals are dedicated to learning other nonstrategic but highly underrepresented languages. Such groups could be engineered to ensure that, regardless of the demands of the future, personnel who speak a given language are already available to meet the need.[8]

Teasing apart the various outcomes helps clarify which ones are best addressed through language commissioning policies and which are better addressed in other ways.

These outcomes differ from one another in the policies likely to be required for success. Also, any given outcome will most likely require multiple supporting polices. Tailoring each policy to the specific outcome also significantly increases the likelihood of success. Each objective will thus also require distinct lines of funding and oversight.

Make Language Requirements for Commissioning Flexible, and Include a Variety of Incentives and Opportunities

The Air Force has some 65,000 officers on many different career tracks, performing a wide variety of jobs. With all these people engaged in different occupations and with varying backgrounds, interests, and aptitudes, the one-size-fits-all policy of having all incoming officers language proficient at a 3/3 or even a 2/2 by 2016 is unrealistic. Our data underscore that a policy to achieve universal competency among all officers in either the near or distant future not only would demand significant investments in resources, time, and effort but would also not yield enough candidates able to meet the requirement. In addition, in light of the demands of the standard four-year college curriculum, a minimum of five semesters of language study would be a substantial additional burden on undergraduates.

Therefore, our second recommendation is that commissioning requirements for language proficiency be flexible enough that most potential candidates could reasonably meet them and should include a variety of minimum requirements and incentives that accommodate and reward multiple levels of capability. This approach would be more effective in the short term because it would encourage language learning in both advanced language learners and beginners and those with competing academic priorities, such as engineers.

The following are examples of multiple approaches that could, in combination, serve as a comprehensive multipronged language commissioning policy:

---

[8]   One of the most frequent reasons for language attrition is lack of use, generally due to a lack of persons with whom to practice. By intentionally creating and managing language-specific groups, the Air Force can engineer communities in each language that can be tapped for use in practice and maintenance efforts.

1. The Air Force could target and offer scholarships or other incentives to those major-ing or minoring in a language to bring in larger numbers of officers highly proficient in a second language. More college students might be encouraged to choose a second or third language as a minor or major if doing so enhanced their opportunities for commissioning or if their tuition were covered.[9] In these cases, establishing proficiency minimums for commissioning would be appropriate, provided that the expectations for minors were lower than those for majors and that the minimums differed according to language difficulty. For example, requiring a minimum of a 2+/2+ for those majoring in French, a relatively easy language, might be both appropriate and achievable for nearly all French majors; French minors might be expected to score only a 1/1. On the other hand, those majoring in Mandarin, a much more difficult language, might be expected to achieve only a 1/0+ (in listening and reading, respectively), and minors might be safe at a 0+/0.[10]

2. Offering commissioning bonuses to anyone entering with skills in certain languages could serve as a powerful incentive for everyone else. The amount should depend on demonstrated proficiency and should be higher for rare (or strategically important) lan-guages. To encourage relative beginners, a bonus program could reward even low levels of proficiency.

3. Providing flexible, online language training courses for ROTC cadets could also be a way to help them fulfill the requirement. Given that many college students might not be able to fit a language minor into their schedules and that courses in strategic lan-guages might not be available at many schools, such a flexible alternative would make second-language learning more feasible. DLI might provide such courses, and as an incentive, participants could receive bonuses as they progressed through the program.

4. Many undergraduates, such as engineering majors, might not be able to dedicate enough time to language learning, even with flexible learning opportunities. The Air Force could address this challenge by providing additional time and resources that did not interfere with or detract from the requirements of four-year degree programs. For example, the goal of a 2/2 might be achievable for students in any major, even engi-neers, if the Air Force offered an additional year or more of study to be spent entirely on language-intensive coursework and immersion experiences. Although a one-year exten-sion program might not appeal to everyone, our survey found that most officers would have been willing to take a language. They did, however, agree that taking extra lan-guage courses might have distracted from their major or other classes. Our survey also found that many officers viewed the option of being able to spend an extra year in col-lege to study a language favorably.

5. The Air Force could require everyone to get at least some language exposure by com-pleting at least two college-level semesters (or the equivalent) in a second language. This would not be expected to result in any appreciable gain in language proficiency, espe-cially since the courses could be completed by freshmen and the skills never practiced again. However, it would lay a foundation for future training efforts and, at a minimum,

---

[9] Scholarships for foreign-language majors have been available through ROTC in the recent past.

[10] Note that these levels are presented only to illustrate how they can and should vary. Sources at DLI could better predict what would be reasonable for majors and minors in each language, and the requirements should be revisited after any policy is implemented to see if any goals are too difficult or too easy for college students to meet.

would give everyone some language experience. Students would be offered incentives to take less commonly taught but strategically important languages. One added benefit of this requirement, when combined with bonuses for different proficiency levels, would be that some might decide to take additional semesters or maintain what they already learned to earn a commissioning bonus. The Air Force could also further encourage continued study by covering ROTC cadets' tuition costs for any language courses taken beyond the two semesters.

6. The Air Force could also offer immersion opportunities to those studying a language. Consistent with past research, our data show that those with both classroom and immersion experience reached higher levels of proficiency. Therefore, immersion opportunities should be made available and be accommodated during college. For ROTC, this would mean ensuring that summer immersion is allowable within the ROTC training curriculum. The Air Force would need to modify the program to allow students to leave for extended periods and still be able to meet the other ROTC training demands.

7. Finally, the policy should recognize that some candidates might need to be allowed to enter with no language proficiency and/or no language coursework. It might be a tall order to expect officers earning specialized graduate degrees (such as medical doctors and attorneys) to learn a second language in addition to their other requirements. Similar exceptions might be needed to ensure meeting recruiting needs for certain majors, such as engineers. It would be important to accommodate exceptions for these and other special groups of candidates as needed.

The following are some examples that, when combined, would create a well-balanced and flexible set of language commissioning policies:

- offering scholarships for majoring or minoring in a language
- offering commissioning bonuses for varying levels of proficiency
- providing distance learning courses in strategic languages for ROTC cadets
- paying for some to spend an extra year in college to concentrate on language study
- requiring two college semesters of language for commissioning, then paying tuition for language courses beyond two semesters
- making more immersion programs available to ROTC students
- accommodating waivers and exceptions within the policy for certain groups.

This list is not exhaustive. Implementing a varied menu of such options would provide the flexibility needed to ensure that the Air Force can fulfill its wide variety of other commissioning needs yet would still provide a host of incentives to increase the depth and range of language skills of new officers overall.

This approach would, however, require significant oversight to manage and implement the multiple commissioning policies. Moreover, many of the policies would require dedicated funds and staff (e.g., scholarships, commissioning bonuses, and providing distance learning courses).

Implement Policies for Maintaining and Enhancing Language Skills

Language skills, when left idle, deteriorate quickly (Weltens, 1987). For this reason, any language policy aimed at having certain levels of proficiency at commissioning should be accompanied by a plan for maintaining that proficiency after commissioning. Therefore, career-long language development should be a vital component of Air Force language policy.

Many of our recommendations for career-long language development are similar to those for commissioning. For example, we recommend including multiple types and levels of incentives for improvement and making time and opportunities available for training. One incentive would be to link skills to career outcomes. An important finding of our survey was that, while officers considered language skills important, the majority saw them as unrelated to career success. This revealed that officers do not currently see a positive connection between language skills and career outcomes. Currently, second-language skills play no role in performance evaluations. For that reason, if learning a second language takes time away from primary duties, it can actually hinder promotion outcomes. If the Air Force intends to encourage second-language learning and maintenance, it must align career incentives with these goals, encourage officers to pursue training, and make it possible to participate in training without hindering career progress.

Another incentive would be to offer additional pay for higher language proficiency. Pay for proficiency does exist in the Air Force in the form of the Foreign Language Proficiency Bonus. In its current form, however, the bonus does not provide optimum incentives for language development; it is currently available only for high levels of proficiency (typically 2/2 or higher) and is higher for in-demand and strategic languages (DoD Instruction 7280.03, 2007). The idea of increasing pay for increasing levels of language proficiency is good; unfortunately, payment starts at such advanced levels of proficiency that someone who is just starting out would not qualify for the bonus for many years. This incentive is thus enticing only to those who already have high levels of proficiency. Adding a series of lower-level bonuses to reward lower-level skills would be more likely to encourage those at more basic levels.

As an alternative to broadening the range of skills supported by the Foreign Langauge Proficiency Pay program or as a supplement, the Air Force could also consider offering bonuses to individuals participating in a structured language training program. Participants could receive bonuses for demonstrating incremental improvement at predetermined points in the training program. For example, if the Air Force provided language instruction once a week for a three years, the program could establish the proficiency levels that would earn bonuses at set intervals, such as 6, 12, 18, 24, 30, and 36 months. Those performing at high levels at the six-month interval would receive the highest bonus amount (say $1,000); those at slightly lower levels would receive a lower amount (say $500), and those at the lowest levels get a still lower amount (say $250). Another goal tied to varying levels of bonuses (say, $1,000 and $500 and $250) would then be set for the next six-month mark.

Our next suggestion is to provide language training to officers during work hours or when spouses can participate. Many survey respondents found these to be the most attractive options for language learning. While language training along with immersion tours could be voluntary for well-established officers, mandatory training for new officers also makes sense.[11] Requiring all officers to attend language training once a week for the first four years of their careers would quickly realize the vision of having them all attain 2/2 proficiency. More important,

---

[11] Note that a voluntary career-long language training program, Language Enabled Airman Program (LEAP), is under way in the Air Force (for more information, see McKeen, 2010). However, due to resource constraints, the program can accommodate only a small handful of highly qualified individuals. We would recommend vastly expanding the number of people who are qualified to participate.

instituting mandatory language training would allow the Air Force to control and manage the overall flow and inventory of languages. Combined with an incentive structure for achieving incremental proficiency levels, such a policy, although very expensive to implement, would be a recipe for success.

Officers in our survey also expressed concerns about lack of opportunities to utilize language skills while serving (see, for example, the survey write-in comments in Appendix F). The Air Force does have career fields for which language skills would be pertinent, such as regional affairs specialists and political affairs specialists, but few people are engaged in jobs that can use these skills. If individuals were offered opportunities to take on temporary duty assignments that utilized their language skills, many would likely take advantage of them, particularly if such assignments were viewed favorably in promotions. It is worth noting again that, at present, assignments geared toward foreign-language skills tend to be disadvantageous for career progression in the Air Force or, at best, considered a diversion. Offering foreign-language assignments and making them advantageous to officers will motivate interest in gaining language proficiency and allow the Air Force to actually leverage the language skills of its officers. Such leveraging of existing skills in job assignments will make the needed investments in building language proficiency actually pay off.

A final suggestion is to improve Air Force personnel data system records on current and past language proficiency and use them in making job assignments. At present, only current (not past) DLPT scores are on record, and then only for those who choose to test. Because high levels of proficiency are required for the Foreign Language Proficiency Bonus, those who would not be likely to qualify typically do not attempt the test and, therefore, are not recorded in the current personnel data system. In addition, not all personnel are assessed for language aptitude, and language preferences and interests are not on record.[12]

The potential benefits of these policies would include promoting career-long development of language skills and, in turn, enhance the success of language commissioning policies. However, if precommissioning efforts are not linked with such development efforts, language commissioning policies may not yield long-lasting improvements in officer proficiency.

Commissioning policies and career-long development policies are overseen by different Air Force agencies; cooperation among these agencies is vital for the success of this recommendation.

Ensure Buy-In from Air Force Officers at All Levels

Research has shown that what an individual believes about a skill's importance to his or her career can affect whether efforts to develop that skill are effective (for a review, see Yamnill and McLean, 2001, and Burke and Hutchins, 2007). Our survey showed that, while officers tended to agree that language capability is important for the warfighting mission, they tended to see it as much less relevant to their own jobs and careers. This finding suggests that, even if language development were made mandatory, the lack of buy-in for an officer's personal career success may hinder the success of development efforts. The best way to mitigate that possibility would be to launch an Air Force–wide campaign to change officers' views about the relevance of a second language to all jobs and to back that up by tying that skill directly to important career outcomes, including promotions. Using language skills as a positive factor in promotion

---

[12] It is worth noting that many of our survey respondents voiced a strong desire to participate in language training. There should be an official record of that interest.

decisions would dispel lingering sentiments that these skills are not personally relevant. Until the Air Force makes such changes, these views are likely to continue and to affect language-learning motivation.

Making language training widely available, providing time to attend development courses and immersion programs during the regular workday, and offering incentives and extra pay for continuously developing those skills (even at initially low levels) would send a strong signal to personnel about just how important these skills are to the Air Force. Conversely, failing to provide those incentives, resources, and opportunities sends the opposite message.

Some possible strong positive signals include

- establishing clear rewards for success
- tying language proficiency to performance evaluations and career outcomes
- making language training programs widely available
- providing time to attend development courses
- making immersion programs available during the regular workday
- offering incentives and extra pay for continuous skill development (even at initially low levels).

A clear and consistent message will require coordination, cooperation, and buy-in from many levels of Air Force leadership. However, only minimal resources would be required beyond those discussed in earlier recommendations.

Evaluate the Success of Each New Program, and Adjust the Program Accordingly

Based on our review of the literature and the results of our survey, we recommend that the Air Force use multiple approaches to maximize its success in increasing the language proficiency of its officers. However, many questions about those approaches remain. How should the Air Force decide who is best suited for immersion programs? How much time each week or month should officers be given to practice and maintain their skills? How often should they be tested to ensure that they are not losing the skills they have? How much additional pay is enough to motivate learning and make less-studied, more-difficult languages attractive? In this sense, more research is clearly needed.

However, the most informative research efforts will be those that (1) occur after concerted attempts have been made to begin implementing new language programs and (2) involve a continuous and systematic process of evaluating and informing changes to the new programs. That process should involve the following steps:

- Detail all the desired outcomes or objectives of a given program and prepare an official statement describing them (examples include improved attitudes toward other cultures, improved language proficiency, improved interest in language development).
- Design and implement a program or set of programs to achieve the specified objectives (such as taking classes during work hours, adding a commissioning requirement, or providing incentives for maintenance).
- Evaluate the effectiveness of the program(s). Measure a variety of consequences including those specifically stated to be outcomes of the program (examples include measuring officer reactions to the program, changes in proficiency levels, and rates of participation). Compare the success of the program across participants and modify aspects of

the program to determine which components are most successful at meeting the stated objectives.

- Specify other research questions that need to be addressed (e.g., Who should be given the opportunity to participate in this program? How should they be selected to participate?) and pursue them.
- Modify the program(s) using information gleaned from the research.
- Institutionalize career-long assessments as checks to confirm that the programs are working as intended (e.g., establish mandatory language proficiency testing every few years to measure language maintenance and improvement). Examine the results of the assessments to identify new training needs every few years.
- Identify training needs and use them to establish new programs or to modify the existing programs and repeat the steps described above.

This repeated process of specifying objectives, developing programs, evaluating the outcomes of the programs, and modifying the policies based on that research is the cornerstone of any well-designed performance improvement intervention. As such, it should drive the development of all future Air Force language policies.

Such research efforts would serve to clarify the goals and quantify the success of each program. That information, in turn, would lead to modification or termination of unsuccessful programs. These efforts would also allow continuous assessment of training needs and gaps and could be used to drive policy changes.

These efforts could also help save resources by concentrating them on programs with proven track records, experimental programs aimed at improving success, and new programs intended to fill training gaps.

Next Steps

The following are the key immediate next steps for establishing Air Force policy for ensuring a language-enabled officer force:

- Produce a detailed policy statement clearly defining all the intended outcomes and goals of language policies, taking care to distinguish the aims of developing language professionals from the aims of developing a language-enabled officer force.
- Implement several precommissioning language opportunities. For each, produce an official statement specifying which specific goal(s) or outcome(s) (from those outlined in the policy statement) the opportunity is aimed at achieving.
- Implement postcommissioning language maintenance and development programs aimed directly at continuing and improving development resulting from the precommissioning policies. For each produce an official statement specifying which specific goal(s) or outcome(s) (from those outlined in the policy statement) the opportunity is aimed at achieving.
- Implement new policies tying language outcomes to career success and institute a campaign to gain buy-in at all levels of the Air Force about the importance of language proficiency for each and every Air Force job.

- Conduct research examining the effectiveness of each new precommissioning program and postcommissioning program at achieving its stated goals and evaluating the success of efforts to gain buy-in. Make changes to programs and policies based on the results of that research.

Closing Comment

Many official DoD and Air Force sources describe language skills as a key warfighting competency.[13] Given the clear consensus that language skills are important, there is little argument that the spirit of our sponsor's vision, establishing a language-proficient officer force, is a worthwhile aim for the Air Force. The results of our study do not diminish the value of that vision. Instead, our results identify the most effective, efficient, and realistic means for achieving that vision and show that there are important trade-offs that would occur in striving to meet it that must be considered. We hope this study will stimulate discussion about those trade-offs and help the Air Force meet its call for a language-enabled force.

---

[13] See, for instance, DoD, 2005; U.S. Air Force, 2009; and DoD, 2010.

Interagency Language Roundtable Language Skill Level Descriptions

ILR provides a set of detailed descriptions for its speaking, reading, and listening proficiency levels. The following material was retrieved from the ILR website on April 26, 2012, and is reproduced verbatim from the pages cited.

Reading[1]

Preface The following proficiency level descriptions characterize comprehension of the written language. Each of the six "base levels" implies control of any previous "base level's" functions and accuracy. The "plus level" designation will be assigned when proficiency substantially exceeds one base skill level and does not fully meet the criteria for the next "base level." The "plus level" descriptions are therefore supplementary to the "base level" descriptions. A skill level is assigned to a person through an authorized language examination.

Examiners assign a level on a variety of performance criteria exemplified in the descriptive statements. Therefore, the examples given here illustrate, but do not exhaustively describe, either the skills a person may possess or situations in which he/she may function effectively. Statements describing accuracy refer to typical stages in the development of competence in the most commonly taught languages in formal training programs. In other languages, emerging competence parallels these characterizations, but often with different details.

Unless otherwise specified, the term "native reader" refers to native readers of a standard dialect. "Well-educated," in the context of these proficiency descriptions, does not necessarily imply formal higher education. However, in cultures where formal higher education is common, the language-use abilities of persons who have had such education is considered the standard. That is, such a person meets contemporary expectations for the formal, careful style of the language, as well as a range of less formal varieties of the language.

In the following descriptions a standard set of text-types is associated with each level. The text-type is generally characterized in each descriptive statement. The word "read," in the context of these proficiency descriptions, means that the person at a given skill level can thoroughly understand the communicative intent in the text-types described. In the usual case the reader could be expected to make a full representation, thorough summary, or translation of the text into English. Other useful operations can be performed on written texts that do not require the ability to "read" as defined above. Examples of such tasks which people of a given skill level may reasonably be expected to perform are provided, when appropriate, in the descriptions.

---

[1] This section is taken from ILR, 2011d, retrieved April 26, 2012, and is used with permission.

R-0: Reading 0 (No Proficiency) No practical ability to read the language. Consistently misunderstands or cannot comprehend at all.

R-0+: Reading 0+ (Memorized Proficiency) Can recognize all the letters in the printed version of an alphabetic system and high-frequency elements of a syllabary or a character system. Able to read some or all of the following: numbers, isolated words and phrases, personal and place names, street signs, office and shop designations. The above often interpreted inaccurately. Unable to read connected prose.

R-1: Reading 1 (Elementary Proficiency) Sufficient comprehension to read very simple connected written material in a form equivalent to usual printing or typescript. Can read either representations of familiar formulaic verbal exchanges or simple language containing only the highest frequency structural patterns and vocabulary, including shared international vocabulary items and cognates (when appropriate). Able to read and understand known language elements that have been recombined in new ways to achieve different meanings at a similar level of simplicity. Texts may include descriptions of persons, places or things: and explanations of geography and government such as those simplified for tourists. Some misunderstandings possible on simple texts. Can get some main ideas and locate prominent items of professional significance in more complex texts. Can identify general subject matter in some authentic texts.

R-1+: Reading 1+ (Elementary Proficiency, Plus) Sufficient comprehension to understand simple discourse in printed form for informative social purposes. Can read material such as announcements of public events, simple prose containing biographical information or narration of events, and straightforward newspaper headlines. Can guess at unfamiliar vocabulary if highly contextualized, but with difficulty in unfamiliar contexts. Can get some main ideas and locate routine information of professional significance in more complex texts. Can follow essential points of written discussion at an elementary level on topics in his/her special professional field. In commonly taught languages, the individual may not control the structure well. For example, basic grammatical relations are often misinterpreted, and temporal reference may rely primarily on lexical items as time indicators. Has some difficulty with the cohesive factors in discourse, such as matching pronouns with referents. May have to read materials several times for understanding.

R-2: Reading 2 (Limited Working Proficiency) Sufficient comprehension to read simple, authentic written material in a form equivalent to usual printing or typescript on subjects within a familiar context. Able to read with some misunderstandings straightforward, familiar, factual material, but in general insufficiently experienced with the language to draw inferences directly from the linguistic aspects of the text. Can locate and understand the main ideas and details in material written for the general reader. However, persons who have professional knowledge of a subject may be able to summarize or perform sorting and locating tasks with written texts that are well beyond their general proficiency level. The individual can read uncomplicated, but authentic prose on familiar subjects that are normally presented in a predictable sequence which aids the reader in understanding. Texts may include descriptions and narrations in contexts such as news items describing frequently occurring events, simple biographical information, social notices, formulaic business letters, and simple technical material written for the general reader. Generally the prose that can be read by the individual is predominantly in straightforward/high-frequency sentence patterns. The individual does not have a broad active vocabulary (that is, which he/she recognizes immediately on sight), but is able to use contextual and real-world cues to understand the text. Characteristically, however, the individual is quite slow in performing such a process. Is typically able to answer factual questions about authentic texts of the types described above.

R-2+: Reading 2+ (Limited Working Proficiency, Plus) Sufficient comprehension to understand most factual material in non-technical prose as well as some discussions on concrete topics related to special professional interests. Is markedly more proficient at reading materials on a familiar topic. Is able to separate the main ideas and details from lesser ones and uses that distinction to advance understanding. The individual is able to use linguistic context and real-world knowledge to make sensible guesses about unfamiliar material. Has a broad active reading vocabulary. The individual is able to get the gist of main and subsidiary ideas in texts which could only be read thoroughly by persons with much higher proficiencies. Weaknesses include slowness, uncertainty, inability to discern nuance and/or intentionally disguised meaning.

R-3: Reading 3 (General Professional Proficiency) Able to read within a normal range of speed and with almost complete comprehension a variety of authentic prose material on unfamiliar subjects. Reading ability is not dependent on subject matter knowledge, although it is not expected that the individual can comprehend thoroughly subject matter which is highly dependent on cultural knowledge or which is outside his/her general experience and not accompanied by explanation. Text-types include news stories similar to wire service reports or international news items in major periodicals, routine correspondence, general reports, and technical material in his/her professional field; all of these may include hypothesis, argumentation and supported opinions. Misreading rare. Almost always able to interpret material correctly, relate ideas and "read between the lines" (that is, understand the writers' implicit intents in text of the above types). Can get the gist of more sophisticated texts, but may be unable to detect or understand subtlety and nuance. Rarely has to pause over or reread general vocabulary. However, may experience some difficulty with unusually complex structure and low frequency idioms.

R-3+: Reading 3+ (General Professional Proficiency, Plus) Can comprehend a variety of styles and forms pertinent to professional needs. Rarely misinterprets such texts or rarely experiences difficulty relating ideas or making inferences. Able to comprehend many sociolinguistic and cultural references. However, may miss some nuances and subtleties. Able to comprehend a considerable range of intentionally complex structures, low frequency idioms, and uncommon connotative intentions, however, accuracy is not complete. The individual is typically able to read with facility, understand, and appreciate contemporary expository, technical or literary texts which do not rely heavily on slang and unusual items.

R-4: Reading 4 (Advanced Professional Proficiency) Able to read fluently and accurately all styles and forms of the language pertinent to professional needs. The individual's experience with the written language is extensive enough that he/she is able to relate inferences in the text to real-world knowledge and understand almost all sociolinguistic and cultural references. Able to "read beyond the lines" (that is, to understand the full ramifications of texts as they are situated in the wider cultural, political, or social environment). Able to read and understand the intent of writers' use of nuance and subtlety. The individual can discern relationships among sophisticated written materials in the context of broad experience. Can follow unpredictable turns of thought readily in, for example, editorial, conjectural, and literary texts in any subject matter area directed to the general reader. Can read essentially all materials in his/her special field, including official and professional documents and correspondence. Recognizes all professionally relevant vocabulary known to the educated non-professional native, although may have some difficulty with slang. Can read reasonably legible handwriting without difficulty. Accuracy is often nearly that of a well-educated native reader.

R-4+: Reading 4+ (Advanced Professional Proficiency, Plus) Nearly native ability to read and understand extremely difficult or abstract prose, a very wide variety of vocabulary, idioms, colloquialisms and slang. Strong sensitivity to and understanding of sociolinguistic and cultural references. Little difficulty in reading less than fully legible handwriting. Broad ability to "read beyond the lines" (that is, to understand the full ramifications of texts as they are situated in the wider cultural, political, or social environment) is nearly that of a well-read or well-educated native reader. Accuracy is close to that of the well-educated native reader, but not equivalent.

R-5: Reading 5 (Functionally Native Proficiency) Reading proficiency is functionally equivalent to that of the well-educated native reader. Can read extremely difficult and abstract prose; for example, general legal and technical as well as highly colloquial writings. Able to read literary texts, typically including contemporary avant-garde prose, poetry and theatrical writing. Can read classical/archaic forms of literature with the same degree of facility as the well-educated, but non-specialist native. Reads and understands a wide variety of vocabulary and idioms, colloquialisms, slang, and pertinent cultural references. With varying degrees of difficulty, can read all kinds of handwritten documents. Accuracy of comprehension is equivalent to that of a well-educated native reader.

Speaking[2]

Preface The following proficiency level descriptions characterize spoken language use. Each of the six "base levels" (coded 00, 10, 20, 30, 40, and 50) implies control of any previous "base level's" functions and accuracy. The "plus level" designation (coded 06, 16, 26, etc.) will be assigned when proficiency substantially exceeds one base skill level and does not fully meet the criteria for the next "base level." The "plus level" descriptions are therefore supplementary to the "base level" descriptions. A skill level is assigned to a person through an authorized language examination. Examiners assign a level on a variety of performance criteria exemplified in the descriptive statements. Therefore, the examples given here illustrate, but do not exhaustively describe, either the skills a person may possess or situations in which he/she may function effectively. Statements describing accuracy refer to typical stages in the development of competence in the most commonly taught languages in formal training programs. In other languages, emerging competence parallels these characterizations, but often with different details. Unless otherwise specified, the term "native speaker" refers to native speakers of a standard dialect. "Well-educated," in the context of these proficiency descriptions, does not necessarily imply formal higher education; however, in cultures where formal higher education is common, the language-use abilities of persons who have had such education is considered the standard. That is, such a person meets contemporary expectations for the formal, careful style of the language, as well as a range of less formal varieties of the language.

Speaking 0 (No Proficiency) Unable to function in the spoken language. Oral production is limited to occasional isolated words. Has essentially no communicative ability. (Has been coded L-0 in some nonautomated applications.) [Data Code 0]

---

2   This section is taken from ILR, 2011e, retrieved April 26, 2012, and is used with permission.

Speaking 0+ (Memorized Proficiency) Able to satisfy immediate needs using rehearsed utterances. Shows little real autonomy of expression, flexibility or spontaneity. Can ask questions or make statements with reasonable accuracy only with memorized utterances or formulae. Attempts at creating speech are usually unsuccessful. Examples: The individual's vocabulary is usually limited to areas of immediate survival needs.

Most utterances are telegraphic; that is, functors (linking words, markers and the like) are omitted, confused or distorted. An individual can usually differentiate most significant sounds when produced in isolation but, when combined in words or groups of words, errors may be frequent. Even with repetition, communication is severely limited even with people used to dealing with foreigners. Stress, intonation, tone, etc. are usually quite faulty. (Has been coded S-0+ in some nonautomated applications.) [Data Code 06]

Speaking 1 (Elementary Proficiency) Able to satisfy minimum courtesy requirements and maintain very simple face-to-face conversations on familiar topics. A native speaker must often use slowed speech, repetition, paraphrase, or a combination of these to be understood by this individual. Similarly, the native speaker must strain and employ real-world knowledge to understand even simple statements/questions from this individual. This speaker has a functional, but limited proficiency. Misunderstandings are frequent, but the individual is able to ask for help and to verify comprehension of native speech in face-to-face interaction. The individual is unable to produce continuous discourse except with rehearsed material. Examples: Structural accuracy is likely to be random or severely limited. Time concepts are vague. Vocabulary is inaccurate, and its range is very narrow. The individual often speaks with great difficulty. By repeating, such speakers can make themselves understood to native speakers who are in regular contact with foreigners but there is little precision in the information conveyed. Needs, experience or training may vary greatly from individual to individual; for example, speakers at this level may have encountered quite different vocabulary areas. However, the individual can typically satisfy predictable, simple, personal and accommodation needs; can generally meet courtesy, introduction, and identification requirements; exchange greetings; elicit and provide, for example, predictable and skeletal biographical information. He/she might give information about business hours, explain routine procedures in a limited way. and state in a simple manner what actions will be taken. He/she is able to formulate some questions even in languages with complicated question constructions. Almost every utterance may be characterized by structural errors and errors in basic grammatical relations. Vocabulary is extremely limited and characteristically does not include modifiers. Pronunciation, stress, and intonation are generally poor, often heavily influenced by another language. Use of structure and vocabulary is highly imprecise. (Has been coded S-1 in some nonautomated applications.) [Data Code 10]

Speaking 1+ (Elementary Proficiency, Plus) Can initiate and maintain predictable face-to-face conversations and satisfy limited social demands. He/she may, however, have little understanding of the social conventions of conversation. The interlocutor is generally required to strain and employ real-world knowledge to understand even some simple speech. The speaker at this level may hesitate and may have to change subjects due to lack of language resources. Range and control of the language are limited. Speech largely consists of a series of short, discrete utterances. Examples: The individual is able to satisfy most travel and accommodation needs and a limited range of social demands beyond exchange of skeletal biographic information. Speaking ability may extend beyond immediate survival needs. Accuracy in basic grammatical relations is evident, although not consistent. May exhibit the more common forms of verb tenses, for example, but may make frequent errors in formation and selection. While some structures are established, errors occur in more complex patterns. The individual typically cannot sustain coherent structures in longer utterances or unfamiliar situations. Ability to describe and give precise information is limited. Person, space and time references are often used incorrectly. Pronunciation is understandable to natives used to dealing with foreigners. Can combine most significant sounds with reasonable comprehensibility, but has difficulty in producing certain sounds in certain positions or in certain combinations. Speech will usually be labored. Frequently has to repeat utterances to be understood by the general public. (Has been coded S-1+ in some nonautomated applications.) [Data Code 16]

Speaking 2 (Limited Working Proficiency) Able to satisfy routine social demands and limited work requirements. Can handle routine work-related interactions that are limited in scope. In more complex and sophisticated work-related tasks, language usage generally disturbs the native speaker. Can handle with confidence, but not with facility, most normal, high-frequency social conversational situations including extensive, but casual conversations about current events, as well as work, family, and autobiographical information. The individual can get the gist of most everyday conversations but has some difficulty understanding native speakers in situations that require specialized or sophisticated knowledge. The individual's utterances are minimally cohesive. Linguistic structure is usually not very elaborate and not thoroughly controlled; errors are frequent. Vocabulary use is appropriate for high-frequency utterances. but unusual or imprecise elsewhere. Examples: While these interactions will vary widely from individual to individual, the individual can typically ask and answer predictable questions in the workplace and give straightforward instructions to subordinates. Additionally, the individual can participate in personal and accommodation-type interactions with elaboration and facility; that is, can give and understand complicated, detailed, and extensive directions and make non-routine changes in travel and accommodation arrangements. Simple structures and basic grammatical relations are typically controlled; however, there are areas of weakness. In the commonly taught languages, these may be simple markings such as plurals, articles, linking words, and negatives or more complex structures such as tense/aspect usage, case morphology. passive constructions, word order, and embedding. (Has been coded S-2 in some nonautomated applications.) [Data Code 20]

Speaking 2+ (Limited Working Proficiency, Plus) Able to satisfy most work requirements with language usage that is often, but not always, acceptable and effective. The individual shows considerable ability to communicate effectively on topics relating to particular interests and special fields of competence. Often shows a high degree of fluency and ease of speech, yet when under tension or pressure, the ability to use the language effectively may deteriorate. Comprehension of normal native speech is typically nearly complete. The individual may miss cultural and local references and may require a native speaker to adjust to his/her limitations in some ways. Native speakers often perceive the individual's speech to contain awkward or inaccurate phrasing of ideas, mistaken time, space and person references, or to be in some way inappropriate, if not strictly incorrect. Examples: Typically the individual can participate in most social, formal, and informal interactions, but limitations either in range of contexts, types of tasks or level of accuracy hinder effectiveness. The individual may be ill at ease with the use of the language either in social interaction or in speaking at length in professional contexts. He/she is generally strong in either structural precision or vocabulary, but not in both. Weakness or unevenness in one of the foregoing, or in pronunciation, occasionally results in miscommunication. Normally controls, but cannot always easily produce general vocabulary. Discourse is often incohesive. (Has been coded S-2+ in some nonautomated applications.) [Data Code 26]

Speaking 3 (General Professional Proficiency) Able to speak the language with sufficient structural accuracy and vocabulary to participate effectively in most formal and informal conversations in practical, social and professional topics. Nevertheless, the individual's limitations generally restrict the professional contexts of language use to matters of shared knowledge and/or international convention. Discourse is cohesive. The individual uses the language acceptably, but with some noticeable imperfections; yet, errors virtually never interfere with understanding and rarely disturb the native speaker. The individual can effectively combine structure and vocabulary to convey his/her meaning accurately. The individual speaks readily and fills pauses suitably. In face-to-face conversation with natives speaking the standard dialect at a normal rate of speech, comprehension is quite complete. Although cultural references, proverbs and the implications of nuances and idiom may not be fully understood, the individual can easily repair the conversation. Pronunciation may be obviously foreign. Individual sounds are accurate: but stress, intonation and pitch control may be faulty. Examples: Can typically discuss particular interests and special fields of competence with reasonable ease. Can use the language as part of normal professional duties such as answering objections, clarifying points, justifying decisions, understanding the essence of challenges, stating and defending policy, conducting meetings, delivering briefings, or other extended and elaborate informative monologues. Can reliably elicit information and informed opinion from native speakers. Structural inaccuracy is rarely the major cause of misunderstanding. Use of structural devices is flexible and elaborate. Without searching for words or phrases, the individual uses the language clearly and relatively naturally to elaborate concepts freely and make ideas easily understandable to native speakers. Errors occur in low-frequency and highly complex structures. (Has been coded S-3 in some nonautomated applications.) [Data Code 30]

Speaking 3+ (General Professional Proficiency, Plus) Is often able to use the language to satisfy professional needs in a wide range of sophisticated and demanding tasks. Examples: Despite obvious strengths, may exhibit some hesitancy, uncertainty, effort or errors which limit the range of language-use tasks that can be reliably performed. Typically there is particular strength in fluency and one or more, but not all, of the following: breadth of lexicon, including low- and medium-frequency items, especially socio-linguistic/cultural references and nuances of close synonyms; structural precision, with sophisticated features that are readily, accurately and appropriately controlled (such as complex modification and embedding in Indo-European languages); discourse competence in a wide range of contexts and tasks, often matching a native speaker's strategic and organizational abilities and expectations. Occasional patterned errors occur in low frequency and highly-complex structures. (Has been coded S-3+ in some nonautomated applications.) [Data Code 36]

Speaking 4 (Advanced Professional Proficiency) Able to use the language fluently and accurately on all levels normally pertinent to professional needs. The individual's language usage and ability to function are fully successful. Organizes discourse well, using appropriate rhetorical speech devices, native cultural references and understanding. Language ability only rarely hinders him/her in performing any task requiring language; yet, the individual would seldom be perceived as a native. Speaks effortlessly and smoothly and is able to use the language with a high degree of effectiveness, reliability and precision for all representational purposes within the range of personal and professional experience and scope of responsibilities. Can serve as in informal interpreter in a range of unpredictable circumstances. Can perform extensive, sophisticated language tasks, encompassing most matters of interest to well-educated native speakers, including tasks which do not bear directly on a professional specialty.

Examples: Can discuss in detail concepts which are fundamentally different from those of the target culture and make those concepts clear and accessible to the native speaker. Similarly, the individual can understand the details and ramifications of concepts that are culturally or conceptually different from his/her own. Can set the tone of interpersonal official, semi-official and non-professional verbal exchanges with a representative range of native speakers (in a range of varied audiences, purposes, tasks and settings). Can play an effective role among native speakers in such contexts as conferences, lectures and debates on matters of disagreement. Can advocate a position at length, both formally and in chance encounters, using sophisticated verbal strategies. Understands and reliably produces shifts of both subject matter and tone. Can understand native speakers of the standard and other major dialects in essentially any face-to-face interaction. (Has been coded S-4 in some non-automated applications.) [Data Code 40]

Speaking 4+ (Advanced Professional Proficiency, Plus) Speaking proficiency is regularly superior in all respects, usually equivalent to that of a well educated, highly articulate native speaker. Language ability does not impede the performance of any language-use task. However, the individual would not necessarily be perceived as culturally native. Examples: The individual organizes discourse well. employing functional rhetorical speech devices, native cultural references and understanding. Effectively applies a native speaker's social and circumstantial knowledge; however, cannot sustain that performance under all circumstances. While the individual has a wide range and control of structure, an occasional nonnative slip may occur. The individual has a sophisticated control of vocabulary and phrasing that is rarely imprecise, yet there are occasional weaknesses in idioms, colloquialisms, pronunciation, cultural reference or there may be an occasional failure to interact in a totally native manner. (Has been coded S-4+ in some nonautomated applications.) [Data Code 46]

Speaking 5 (Functionally Native Proficiency) Speaking proficiency is functionally equivalent to that of a highly articulate well-educated native speaker and reflects the cultural standards of the country where the language is natively spoken. The individual uses the language with complete flexibility and intuition, so that speech on all levels is fully accepted by well-educated native speakers in all of its features, including breadth of vocabulary and idiom, colloquialisms and pertinent cultural references. Pronunciation is typically consistent with that of well-educated native speakers of a non-stigmatized dialect. (Has been coded S-5 in some nonautomated applications.) [Data Code 50]

Listening[3]

Preface The following proficiency level descriptions characterize comprehension of the spoken language. Each of the six "base levels" (coded 00, 10, 20, 30, 40, and 50) implies control of any previous "base levels" functions and accuracy. The "plus level" designation (coded 06, 16, 26, etc.) will be assigned when proficiency substantially exceeds one base skill level and does not fully meet the criteria for the next "base level." The "plus level" descriptions are therefore supplementary to the "base level" descriptions. A skill level is assigned to a person through an authorized language examination. Examiners assign a level

---

[3] This section is taken from ILR, 2011c, retrieved April 26, 2012, and is used with permission.

on a variety of performance criteria exemplified in the descriptive statements. Therefore, the examples given here illustrate, but do not exhaustively describe, either the skills a person may possess or situations in which he/she may function effectively. Statements describing accuracy refer to typical stages in the development of competence in the most commonly taught languages in formal training programs. In other languages, emerging competence parallels these characterizations, but often with different details. Unless otherwise specified, the term "native listener" refers to native speakers and listeners of a standard dialect. "Well-educated," in the context of these proficiency descriptions, does not necessarily imply formal higher education. However, in cultures where formal higher education is common, the language-use abilities of persons who have had such education is considered the standard. That is, such a person meets contemporary expectations for the formal, careful style of the language, as well as a range of less formal varieties of the language.

Listening 0 (No Proficiency) No practical understanding of the spoken language. Understanding is limited to occasional isolated words with essentially no ability to comprehend communication. (Has been coded L-0 in some nonautomated applications.) [Data Code 00]

Listening 0+ (Memorized Proficiency) Sufficient comprehension to understand a number of memorized utterances in areas of immediate needs. Slight increase in utterance length understood but requires frequent long pauses between understood phrases and repeated requests on the listener's part for repetition. Understands with reasonable accuracy only when this involves short memorized utterances or formulae. Utterances understood are relatively short in length. Misunderstandings arise due to ignoring or inaccurately hearing sounds or word endings (both inflectional and non-inflectional), distorting the original meaning. Can understand only with difficulty even such people as teachers who are used to speaking with non-native speakers. Can understand best those statements where context strongly supports the utterance's meaning. Gets some main ideas. (Has been coded L-0+ in some nonautomated applications.) [Data Code 06]

Listening 1 (Elementary Proficiency) Sufficient comprehension to understand utterances about basic survival needs and minimum courtesy and travel requirements in areas of immediate need or on very familiar topics, can understand simple questions and answers, simple statements and very simple face-to-face conversations in a standard dialect. These must often be delivered more clearly than normal at a rate slower than normal with frequent repetitions or paraphrase (that is, by a native used to dealing with foreigners). Once learned, these sentences can be varied for similar level vocabulary and grammar and still be understood. In the majority of utterances, misunderstandings arise due to overlooked or misunderstood syntax and other grammatical clues. Comprehension vocabulary inadequate to understand anything but the most elementary needs. Strong interference from the candidate's native language occurs. Little precision in the information understood owing to the tentative state of passive grammar and lack of vocabulary. Comprehension areas include basic needs such as: meals, lodging, transportation, time and simple directions (including both route instructions and orders from customs officials, policemen, etc.). Understands main ideas. (Has been coded L-1 in some nonautomated applications.) [Data Code 10]

Listening 1+ (Elementary Proficiency, Plus) Sufficient comprehension to understand short conversations about all survival needs and limited social demands. Developing flexibility evident in understanding a range of circumstances beyond immediate survival needs. Shows spontaneity in understanding by speed, although consistency of understanding is uneven. Limited vocabulary range necessitates repetition for understanding. Understands more common time forms and most question forms, some word order patterns, but miscommunication still occurs with more complex patterns. Cannot sustain understanding of coherent structures in longer utterances or in unfamiliar situations. Understanding of descriptions and the giving of precise information is limited. Aware of basic cohesive features (e.g., pronouns, verb inflections) but many are unreliably understood, especially if less immediate in reference. Understanding is largely limited to a series of short, discrete utterances. Still has to ask for utterances to be repeated. Some ability to understand facts. (Has been coded L-1+ in some nonautomated applications.) [Data Code 16]

Listening 2 (Limited Working Proficiency) Sufficient comprehension to understand conversations on routine social demands and limited job requirements. Able to understand face-to-face speech in a standard dialect, delivered at a normal rate with some repetition and rewording, by a native speaker not used to dealing with foreigners, about everyday topics, common personal and family news, well-known current events and routine office matters through descriptions and narration about current, past and future events; can follow essential points of discussion or speech at an elementary level on topics in his/her special professional field. Only understands occasional words and phrases of statements made in unfavorable conditions, for example through loudspeakers outdoors. Understands factual content. Native language causes less interference in listening comprehension. Able to understand facts; i.e., the lines but not between or beyond the lines. (Has been coded L-2 in some nonautomated applications.) [Data Code 20]

Listening 2+ (Limited Working Proficiency, Plus) Sufficient comprehension to understand most routine social demands and most conversations on work requirements as well as some discussions on concrete topics related to particular interests and special fields of competence. Often shows remarkable ability and ease of understanding, but under tension or pressure may break down. Candidate may display weakness or deficiency due to inadequate vocabulary base or less than secure knowledge of grammar and syntax. Normally understands general vocabulary with some hesitant understanding of everyday vocabulary still evident. Can sometimes detect emotional overtones. Some ability to understand implications. (Has been coded L-2+ in some nonautomated applications.) [Data Code 26]

Listening 3 (General Professional Proficiency) Able to understand the essentials of all speech in a standard dialect including technical discussions within a special field. Has effective understanding of face-to-face speech, delivered with normal clarity and speed in a standard dialect on general topics and areas of special interest; understands hypothesizing and supported opinions. Has broad enough vocabulary that rarely has to ask for paraphrasing or explanation. Can follow accurately the essentials of conversations between educated native speakers, reasonably clear telephone calls, radio broadcasts, news stories similar to wire service reports, oral reports, some oral technical reports and public addresses on non-technical subjects; can understand without difficulty all forms of standard speech concerning a special professional field. Does not understand native speakers if they speak very quickly or use some slang or dialect. Can often detect emotional overtones. Can understand implications. (Has been coded L-3 in some nonautomated applications.) [Data Code 30]

Listening 3+ (General Professional Proficiency, Plus) Comprehends most of the content and intent of a variety of forms and styles of speech pertinent to professional needs, as well as general topics and social conversation. Ability to comprehend many sociolinguistic and cultural references. However, may miss some subtleties and nuances. Increased ability to comprehend unusually complex structures in lengthy utterances and to comprehend many distinctions in language tailored for different audiences. Increased ability to understand native speakers talking quickly, using nonstandard dialect or slang; however, comprehension is not complete. Can discern some relationships among sophisticated listening materials in the context of broad experience. Can follow some unpredictable turns of thought readily, for example, in informal and formal speeches covering editorial, conjectural and literary material in subject matter areas directed to the general listener. (Has been coded L-3+ in some nonautomated applications.) [Data Code 36]

Listening 4 (Advanced Professional Proficiency) Able to understand all forms and styles of speech pertinent to professional needs. Able to understand fully all speech with extensive and precise vocabulary, subtleties and nuances in all standard dialects on any subject relevant to professional needs within the range of his/her experience, including social conversations; all intelligible broadcasts and telephone calls; and many kinds of technical discussions and discourse. Understands language specifically tailored (including persuasion, representation, counseling and negotiating) to different audiences. Able to understand the essentials of speech in some non-standard dialects. Has difficulty in understanding extreme dialect and slang, also in understanding speech in unfavorable conditions, for example through bad loudspeakers outdoors. Can discern relationships among sophisticated listening materials in the context of broad experience. Can follow unpredictable turns of thought readily, for example, in informal and formal speeches covering editorial, conjectural and literary material in any subject matter directed to the general listener. (Has been coded L-4 in some nonautomated applications.) [Data Code 40]

Listening 4+ (Advanced Professional Proficiency, Plus) Increased ability to understand extremely difficult and abstract speech as well as ability to understand all forms and styles of speech pertinent to professional needs, including social conversations. Increased ability to comprehend native speakers using extreme nonstandard dialects and slang, as well as to understand speech in unfavorable conditions. Strong sensitivity to sociolinguistic and cultural references. Accuracy is close to that of the well-educated native listener but still not equivalent. (Has been coded L-4+ in some nonautomated applications.) [Data Code 46]

Listening 5 (Functionally Native Proficiency) Comprehension equivalent to that of the well-educated native listener. Able to understand fully all forms and styles of speech intelligible to the well-educated native listener, including a number of regional and illiterate dialects, highly colloquial speech and conversations and discourse distorted by marked interference from other noise. Able to understand how natives think as they create discourse. Able to understand extremely difficult and abstract speech. (Has been coded L-5 in some nonautomated applications.) [Data Code 50]

RAND's Self-Assessment Items

The ILR has also produced a set of self-assessment items for speaking, reading, and listening proficiency levels (the originals can be found on the organization's website). With ILR's permission, we used these as a starting point for tailoring a set of items for our own analysis. The following boxes present final text of these items used in our survey. Survey participants were asked to check all statements that were true about their capability in a given language.

Survey Items Based on ILR Self-Assessment Items for Speaking

I can

1. say simple greetings (like "hello" or "good afternoon") and leave-taking expressions (like "goodbye" or "see you later") appropriately.

2. say politeness terms (like "please" or "thank you").

3. count to ten.

4. ask or answer a few simple questions (like "How are you?" "Fine, thank you. And you?" "What is that?" "That is a book.").

5. tell/ask someone how to get from here to a nearby hotel, restaurant, or post office.

6. order a simple meal.

7. arrange for a hotel room or taxi ride.

8. buy a needed item such as groceries, or clothing.

9. ask and answer simple questions about date and place of birth, nationality, marital status, occupation, etc.

10. make social introductions and use greeting and leave-taking expressions.

11. handle conversations about familiar topics in an organized way.

12. describe my present or most recent job or activity in some detail.

13. give detailed information about my family, my house, and my community.

14. give a brief autobiography including immediate plans and hopes.

15. feel confident that when I talk with native speakers on topics such as those mentioned above, they understand me most of the time.

16. take and give simple messages over the telephone, or leave a message on voice mail.

17. describe in detail a person or place that is very familiar to me.

18. report the facts of what I have seen recently on television news or read in the newspaper.

19. talk about a trip or some other everyday event that happened in the recent past or that will happen soon.

20. function effectively in professional or work situations using the language.

21. speak without feeling limited by my vocabulary or command of grammar.

22. easily follow and contribute to a conversation among native speakers.

23. on a social occasion, defend personal opinions about social and cultural topics.

24. in professional discussions, use vocabulary that is extensive and precise enough to enable me to convey my exact meaning.

25. almost always speak without making a grammatical mistake.

26. carry out any job assignment as effectively as if in my native language.

27. persuade someone effectively to take a course of action in a sensitive situation such as to improve his/her health, reverse a decision, or establish a policy.

28. speak with a proficiency that is functionally equivalent to that of a highly articulate well-educated native speaker and reflects the cultural standards of a country where the language is natively spoken.

NOTES: Adapted from source material at ILR, 2011g. Speaking scale items were grouped as follows: items 1 to 4 = ILR less than 0+; items 5 to 10 = ILR 0+ to 1; items 11 to 19 = ILR 1+ to 2; items 20 to 24 = ILR 2+ to 3; items 25 to 28 = ILR 3+ and higher.

Survey Items Based on ILR Self-Assessment Items for Reading

I can read and understand

1. the basic letters, characters, or symbols in the writing system.

2. some words and phrases.

3. a few words in simple, everyday material, such as advertisements.

4. some commonplace words on signs and storefronts.

5. short simple sentences, at least sometimes.

6. the purpose and main meaning of very short, simple texts, such as in printed personal notes, business advertisements, public announcements, maps, etc.

7. very short simple written descriptions of some familiar persons, places, and things, like those found in many tourist pamphlets.

8. texts that consist mainly of straightforward factual language, such as short news reports of events, biographical information, descriptions, or simple technical material.

9. very straightforward reports about current and past events.

10. the main ideas of books or articles on topics I am familiar with (at least most of the time), either because they pertain to my work experience or to topics I am interested in.

11. nearly all of the material in a major daily newspaper published in a city or country with which I am familiar.

12. present-day writing and literature with little or no use of a dictionary.

13. the main ideas and important details of almost all material written within my particular professional field or area of primary interest (e.g., reports, analyses, letters, arguments, etc.).

14. virtually all forms of the written language, including abstract, linguistically complex texts such as specialized articles, essays and literary works, including prose works from earlier periods recognized as masterpieces.

NOTES: Adapted from source material at ILR, 2011h. Reading scale items were grouped as follows: items 1 to 5 = ILR less than 0+; items 6 to 7 = ILR 0+ to 1; items 8 to 10 = ILR 1+ to 2; items 11 to 13 = ILR 2+ to 3; item 14 = ILR 3+ and higher.

Survey Items Based on ILR Self-Assessment Items for Listening

I can understand:

1. simple greetings, such as "hello" and "goodbye."

2. politeness words, such as "please" and "thank you."

3. numbers from 1 to 10.

4. some days of the week or some dates, if spoken slowly and clearly.

5. a few basic questions or short statements (like "Where are you from?" "What time is it?" "I like this."), if they are spoken slowly and clearly.

6. basic directions and instructions, such as how to get to a local store.

7. questions and answers about basic survival needs, such as meals, lodging, transportation and time.

8. routine questions about my job, my immediate family and myself.

9. simple statements about a person's background and occupation.

10. speech about everyday topics, for example common personal and family news, well-known current events, and routine situations at work.

11. uncomplicated stories about current, past and future events.

12. at least some details from announcements made over a loudspeaker.

13. the main idea and basic facts from most short news reports on the radio or television.

14. and accurately follow all conversations among native speakers who are speaking at a normal rate of speech.

15. native speakers nearly always without asking them to paraphrase or explain what they have said.

16. speech in a professional setting concerning my field of expertise or some technical subjects, such as a lecture or a panel discussion.

17. all aspects of speech that involves the use of extensive and precise vocabulary, including subtle distinctions between word choices.

18. all aspects of spoken interactions among native speakers at public gatherings, such as meetings, seminars, task groups or conferences.

19. speech in a way that is fully equivalent to that of a well-educated native listener.

NOTES: Adapted from source material at ILR, 2011f. Listening scale items were grouped as follows: items 1 to 5 = ILR less than 0+; items 6 to 9 = ILR 0+ to 1; items 10 to 13 = ILR 1+ to 2; items 14 to 16 = ILR 2+ to 3; items 17 to 19 = ILR 3+ and higher.

Language Flagship Programs

The institutions listed below possess language flagship programs. Web addresses for the institutions and material related to the programs can be found in the references.

Programs in the United States

- African languages
  - Howard University
- Arabic
  - Michigan State University
  - University of Texas, Austin
  - University of Michigan, Ann Arbor
  - University of Maryland, College Park
  - University of Oklahoma
- Chinese
  - Arizona State University
  - Brigham Young University
  - Indiana University
  - Ohio State University
  - University of Mississippi
  - University of Oregon
  - San Francisco State University
  - University of Rhode Island
  - Western Kentucky University
- Hindi and Urdu
  - University of Texas, Austin
- Korean
  - University of Hawaii, Mānoa
- Persian
  - University of Maryland, College Park
- Russian
  - Bryn Mawr College
  - Portland State University
  - University of California, Los Angeles
  - University of Maryland, College Park
  - University of Wisconsin, Madison

Overseas Partner Institutions

- China
  - Nanjing University
  - Qingdao Center
- Egypt
  - Alexandria University
- India
  - Jaipur Hindi Center
  - Lucknow Urdu Center
- Korea
  - Korea University
- Nigeria
  - Ibadan University
- Russia
  - St. Petersburg State University
- Syria
  - Damascus University
- Tajikistan
  - Tajik State National University
- Tanzania
  - Zanzibar State University (Swahili)

Survey Screenshots

This appendix offers screenshots of the main sections of the survey. We excluded screens that rely on identical questions (e.g., college as opposed to high school course questions) and screens that provided additional explanation for the survey taker (e.g., the initial consent statement and an explanation of why we ask about only three languages in some places).

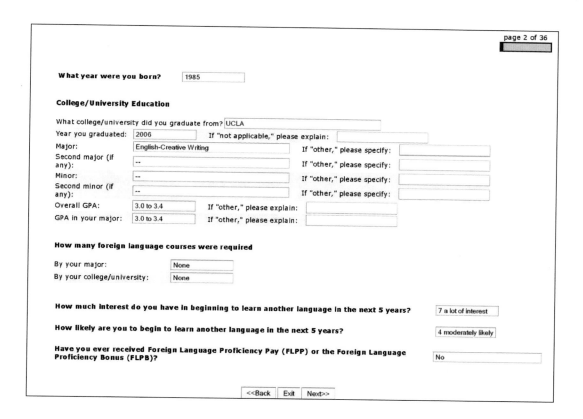

Please list all foreign languages in which you have ever known at least 10 words or more, and the ages at which you first started learning them, starting with the language you currently know best:

If you don't know at least 10 words in any languages, select "none" for the language and NA for the age.

	Language name?	Age you started learning it?
Best language	Chinese - Other (please specify)	Since birth
If "other," please specify:	Wu	
2nd best language	Chinese - Mandarin	2
If "other," please specify:		
3rd best language	French	12
If "other," please specify:		
4th best language	None	NA
If "other," please specify:		

☐ Check here to add more languages

<<Back   Exit   Next>>

Some people have a higher language proficiency at an earlier point in their life, even though they may not have that same proficiency now.

Therefore, please indicate:
A) The HIGHEST level of proficiency that you have EVER had
B) The most recent age that you had that highest level of proficiency
C) Your proficiency in the language NOW

	Level of best proficiency EVER	Most recent age at best proficiency	Proficiency NOW
Wu	Able to speak easily about some complicated topics	25	Able to speak easily about some complicated topics
Chinese - Mandarin	Able to have most everyday conversations with little trouble	24	Able to have simple conversations
French	Able to have simple conversations	17	Enough to have a minimal conversation, if speaking slowly

When did you last use or practice the language?

Wu	Within the last month
Chinese - Mandarin	Within the last 2 years
French	Between 2 and 4 years ago

How many times in your AF career have you been deployed to a location where the local people speak the following languages?

Wu	never
Chinese - Mandarin	never
French	never

<<Back   Exit   Next>>

SPEAKING (For each statement, check if true)

I can:

	Wu	Chinese - Mandarin
(Check here if you can't do any of the things listed below.)	☐	☐
say simple greetings (like "hello" or "good afternoon") and leave-taking expressions (like "goodbye" or "see you later") appropriately.	☒	☒
say politeness terms (like "please" or "thank you").	☒	☒
count to ten.	☒	☒
ask or answer a few simple questions (like "How are you?" "Fine, thank you. And you?" "What is that?" "That is a book.").	☒	☒
tell/ask someone how to get from here to a nearby hotel, restaurant, or post office.	☒	☒
order a simple meal.	☒	☒
arrange for a hotel room or taxi ride.	☒	☒
buy a needed item such as groceries, or clothing.	☒	☒
ask and answer simple questions about date and place of birth, nationality, marital status, occupation, etc.	☒	☒
make social introductions and use greeting and leave-taking expressions.	☒	☒
handle conversations about familiar topics in an organized way.	☒	☒
describe my present or most recent job or activity in some detail.	☒	☒
give detailed information about my family, my house, and my community.	☒	☒
I can give a brief autobiography including immediate plans and hopes.	☒	☒
feel confident that when I talk with native speakers on topics such as those mentioned above, they understand me most of the time.	☒	☐
take and give simple messages over the telephone, or leave a message on voice mail.	☒	☐
describe in detail a person or place that is very familiar to me.	☒	☐
report the facts of what I have seen recently on television news or read in the newspaper.	☐	☐
talk about a trip or some other everyday event that happened in the recent past or that will happen soon.	☒	☒
function effectively in professional or work situations using the language.	☐	☐
speak without feeling limited by my vocabulary or command of grammar.	☐	☐
easily follow and contribute to a conversation among native speakers.	☐	☐
on a social occasion, defend personal opinions about social and cultural topics.	☒	☐
in professional discussions, use vocabulary that is extensive and precise enough to enable me to convey my exact meaning.	☐	☐
almost always speak without making a grammatical mistake.	☐	☐
carry out any job assignment as effectively as if in my native language.	☐	☐
persuade someone effectively to take a course of action in a sensitive situation such as to improve his/her health, reverse a decision, or establish a policy.	☒	☐
speak with a proficiency that is functionally equivalent to that of a highly articulate well-educated native speaker	☐	☐

LISTENING (For each statement, check if true)

I can understand:

	Wu	Chinese - Mandarin
(Check here if you can't do any of the things listed below.)	☐	☐
simple greetings, such as "hello" and "goodbye."	☑	☑
politeness words, such as "please" and "thank you."	☑	☑
numbers from 1 to 10.	☑	☑
some days of the week or some dates, if spoken slowly and clearly.	☑	☑
a few basic questions or short statements (like "Where are you from?" "What time is it?" "I like this."), if they are spoken slowly and clearly.	☑	☑
basic directions and instructions, such as how to get to a local store.	☑	☑
questions and answers about basic survival needs, such as meals, lodging, transportation and time.	☑	☑
routine questions about my job, my immediate family and myself.	☑	☑
simple statements about a person's background and occupation.	☑	☑
speech about everyday topics, for example common personal and family news, well-known current events, and routine situations at work.	☑	☐
uncomplicated stories about current, past and future events.	☑	☑
at least some details from announcements made over a loudspeaker.	☑	☑
the main idea and basic facts from most short news reports on the radio or television.	☐	☑
and accurately follow all conversations among native speakers who are speaking at a normal rate of speech.	☑	☑
native speakers nearly always without asking them to paraphrase or explain what they have said.	☑	☑
speech in a professional setting concerning my field of expertise or some technical subjects, such as a lecture or a panel discussion.	☐	☐
all aspects of speech that involves the use of extensive and precise vocabulary, including subtle distinctions between word choices.	☐	☐
all aspects of spoken interactions among native speakers at public gatherings, such as meetings, seminars, task groups or conferences.	☐	☐
speech in a way that is fully equivalent to that of a well-educated native listener.	☐	☐

<<Back Exit Next>>

READING (For each statement, check if true)

I can read and understand:

	Wu	Chinese - Mandarin
(Check here if you can't do any of the things listed below.)	☐	☐
the basic letters, characters, or symbols in the writing system.	☑	☑
some words and phrases.	☑	☑
a few words in simple, everyday material, such as advertisements.	☑	☑
some commonplace words on signs and storefronts.	☑	☑
short simple sentences, at least sometimes.	☑	☑
the purpose and main meaning of very short, simple texts, such as in printed personal notes, business advertisements, public announcements, maps, etc.	☐	☐
very short simple written descriptions of some familiar persons, places, and things, like those found in many tourist pamphlets.	☐	☐
texts that consist mainly of straightforward factual language, such as short news reports of events, biographical information, descriptions, or simple technical material.	☐	☐
very straightforward reports about current and past events.	☐	☐
the main ideas of books or articles on topics I am familiar with (at least most of the time), either because they pertain to my work experience or to topics I am interested in.	☐	☐
nearly all of the material in a major daily newspaper published in a city or country with which I am familiar.	☐	☐
present-day writing and literature with little or no use of a dictionary.	☐	☐
the main ideas and important details of almost all material written within my particular professional field or area of primary interest (e.g., reports, analyses, letters, arguments, etc.).	☐	☐
virtually all forms of the written language, including abstract, linguistically complex texts such as specialized articles, essays and literary works, including prose works from earlier periods recognized as masterpieces.	☐	☐

<<Back Exit Next>>

Where did you learn the following language(s)? Check all that apply.

	Wu	Chinese - Mandarin	French
Learned it at home as my native language	☑	☐	☐
Learned it at home as one of two or more primary languages in my family	☐	☑	☐
Learned it at home from family members, but it is not my first language	☐	☐	☐
From a caretaker (e.g., nanny)	☐	☐	☐
From friends	☐	☐	☐
Extra-curricular classes and/or activities with my ethnic, heritage, religious or cultural community	☐	☐	☐
Courses in elementary school (including extra-curricular summer classes)	☐	☐	☐
Courses in junior high or middle school (including extra-curricular summer classes)	☐	☐	☑
Courses in high school (including extra-curricular summer classes)	☐	☐	☑
College classroom courses (including USAFA or any other college/university)	☐	☐	☐
Lived and/or worked in a country where the language is spoken	☑	☑	☐
Private tutor (not paid for by employer, military or part of my college/high-school/middle or elementary school education).	☐	☐	☐
Commercial language school (not paid for by employer, military or part of my college/high-school /middle or elementary school education)	☐	☐	☐
Books, computer-based programs or tapes (not paid for by employer, military or part of my college/high-school/middle or elementary school education)	☐	☐	☑
Study abroad program	☐	☐	☐
DLI provided training (including any DLI resource)	☐	☐	☐
Other training provided by the military (not from DLI or USAFA)	☐	☐	☐
A non-military employer provided training	☐	☐	☐
Other (please specify)	☐	☐	☐

<<Back   Exit   Next>>

In HIGH SCHOOL, for how many semesters did you take courses focusing on each of the following areas? (Please count each course only once.)

Include only courses that you completed with a passing grade.

	French
Learning to speak, read and understand the language.	6
Literature (read in the original language)	6
Literature (translated to English)	1
History, art, or cultural norms of regions where the language is spoken	6
Other types of courses (please specify):	--

<<Back   Exit   Next>>

Why did you take the following language(s) in HIGH SCHOOL? Check all that apply.

	French
Speak to friends or family	☐
I thought it would help me get a job and/or further my career	☐
Language courses were required in my school	☑
I thought language skills would be important for my career outside the military	☐
I thought language skills would be important for my career in the military	☐
I had an interest in learning the language for its own sake	☑
Other (please specify)	☐

How have you maintained your skills since taking the courses in HIGH SCHOOL? Check all that apply.

	French
Classroom training	☐
Computer-based or online training program	☐
Textbooks	☐
Audio or video tapes/CDs	☐
Immersion/study abroad program	☐
Lived and/or worked in a country where the language is spoken	☐
Conversing with other people who speak the language	☐
Nothing, I have not done anything to maintain the language	☑
Other (please specify)	☐

<<Back   Exit   Next>>

How much time in total have you spent in countries where the language is spoken?
For example, if you spent 18 months total, you would select 1 year in the "year box" and 6 months in the "months box."

	Years	Months
Wu	4	10
Chinese - Mandarin	4	10

While you were there, what percentage of the time did you use that language for the following activities:

	At work	Running errands or shopping	Commuting or traveling	Socializing with friends	At home
Wu	Never used it	60%	40%	90%	90%
Chinese - Mandarin	Never used it	40%	60%	10%	10%

<<Back   Exit   Next>>

Please indicate how strongly you agree or disagree with the following statements:

	Strongly disagree 1	2	3	Neither agree nor disagree 4	5	6	Strongly agree 7	Decline to answer/NA
I enjoy talking with people from other countries	○	○	○	○	○	○	⊗	○
It is hard to relate to people from other countries	○	○	○	○	○	⊗	○	○
I think languages are interesting	○	○	○	○	○	○	⊗	○
Learning a foreign language is a waste of time	⊗	○	○	○	○	○	○	○
I do not feel comfortable with people from other cultures	○	○	○	⊗	○	○	○	○
I am not interested in learning another language	○	○	○	○	○	○	⊗	○
English is universal, so Americans don't need to learn other languages	○	○	⊗	○	○	○	○	○
Learning languages has always been a challenge for me	○	○	○	○	○	⊗	○	○
I don't really like people who do not speak English	○	○	⊗	○	○	○	○	○
I am interested in other people's cultures	○	○	○	○	○	⊗	○	○
I have always been good at learning languages	○	○	○	○	⊗	○	○	○
Learning foreign languages is worthwhile	○	○	○	○	○	⊗	○	○
I am good at learning new languages	○	○	○	○	⊗	○	○	○
I have a hard time understanding people with foreign accents	○	○	⊗	○	○	○	○	○

<<Back Exit Next>>

Please indicate how strongly you agree or disagree with the following statements:

	Strongly disagree 1	2	3	Neither agree nor disagree 4	5	6	Strongly agree 7	Decline to answer/NA
Knowing a foreign language is important for my Air Force career	○	○	○	○	○	⊗	○	○
Foreign language proficiency is an important warfighting skill	○	○	○	○	○	○	⊗	○
Foreign language ability is not relevant to my job	○	○	○	○	○	⊗	○	○
Knowing math is important for my Air Force career	○	○	○	○	○	○	⊗	○
Knowing a foreign language won't help you get ahead in the Air Force	○	○	⊗	○	○	○	○	○
Knowing U.S. history is important for my Air Force career	○	○	○	⊗	○	○	○	○
All Air Force officers should be required to know a foreign language	○	○	○	○	⊗	○	○	○
Foreign languages are irrelevant to mission success	⊗	○	○	○	○	○	○	○
I just recently developed an interest in learning a foreign language	⊗	○	○	○	○	○	○	○
I wanted to learn a language when I was in college	○	○	○	○	○	⊗	○	○
I have always wanted to learn a foreign language	○	○	○	○	○	○	⊗	○
I have never wanted to learn a foreign language	⊗	○	○	○	○	○	○	○
The older I get, the less I want to learn a foreign language	○	○	○	○	⊗	○	○	○
I wish I had learned a foreign language as a child	○	○	○	○	○	○	○	○
I wish I had started learning a foreign language when I was in 1st grade	○	○	○	○	○	○	⊗	○
It would be good if foreign language proficiency (at a 2/2) were mandatory for promotion to Lt Col	○	○	○	○	⊗	○	○	○

<<Back Exit Next>>

I would be more likely to invest effort in learning another language if:

	Strongly disagree 1	2	3	Neither agree nor disagree 4	5	6	Strongly agree 7	Decline to answer/NA
I would get extra pay for knowing another language	○	○	○	○	○	○	●	○
I would get extra pay while receiving language training	○	○	○	○	○	○	●	○
I could do the language training during my regular work hours	○	○	○	○	○	○	●	○
I could do the language training after my regular work hours so that it wouldn't interfere with my normal AF duties	○	○	○	○	○	○	●	○
Knowing the language meant that I would be assigned to a desirable foreign location	○	○	○	○	○	○	●	○
I could attend an immersion program in a foreign country	○	○	○	○	○	○	●	○
Knowing the language would make me more respected by AF leadership and/or peers	○	○	○	○	○	○	●	○
By knowing the language, I would be viewed more favorably in the AF promotion process	○	○	○	○	○	○	●	○
I could take language classes with my friends or co-workers	○	○	○	○	○	○	○	○
I could take language classes with my spouse	○	○	○	○	○	○	●	○
I could learn it by myself on my own time at my own pace	○	○	○	○	○	○	●	○
I would be learning a language that is useful in the private sector	○	○	○	○	○	○	●	○
The AF would pay for my language training	○	○	○	○	○	○	●	○
Foreign language proficiency were mandatory for promotion to Lt Col	○	○	○	○	○	○	●	○
I would receive other benefits, advantages or rewards, such as (please specify)	○	○	○	○	○	○	●	○

<<Back   Exit   Next>>

I would be concerned about learning another language because I think I might be:

	Strongly disagree 1	2	3	Neither agree nor disagree 4	5	6	Strongly agree 7	Decline to answer/NA
Stovepiped into a certain type of career	○	○	○	○	○	○	●	○
More likely to be deployed outside the US	○	○	○	○	●	○	○	○
More likely to be deployed to a combat zone	○	○	○	●	○	○	○	○
More likely to be sent outside the wire	○	○	○	●	○	○	○	○
Not good at learning languages	○	○	○	○	●	○	○	○
Likely to embarrass myself	○	○	○	●	○	○	○	○
Likely to fail the tests	○	○	○	●	○	○	○	○
Expected to do the training during my personal time	○	○	●	○	○	○	○	○
Required to spend time away from my family during the training	○	○	○	○	●	○	○	○
Required to spend time away from my regular work duties during the training	○	○	○	○	●	○	○	○
Passed over for promotion if I don't focus on my current duties and other professional development opportunities	○	○	○	○	○	●	○	○
Better off doing other work that supports the mission	○	○	○	○	○	●	○	○
Acquiring a useless skill	○	○	○	○	○	●	○	○
Thought of as unpatriotic or un-American	○	○	●	○	○	○	○	○
Likely to have other concerns, such as (please specify)	○	○	○	●	○	○	○	○

<<Back   Exit   Next>>

Thinking back to when you decided to join the AF, do you agree or disagree with the following statements:

	Strongly disagree 1	2	3	Neither agree nor disagree 4	5	6	Strongly agree 7	Decline to answer/NA
I would still have wanted to become an AF officer, even if there had been a foreign language proficiency requirement.	○	○	○	○	○	●	○	○
Knowing the Air Force valued foreign language proficiency would have made me even more interested in becoming an AF officer.	○	○	○	○	○	○	●	○
I would still have wanted to become an AF officer, even if it meant that I had to take foreign language courses in college.	○	○	○	○	○	○	●	○
If the AF had provided an incentive for learning a foreign language while I was in college (such as extra pay), I would have been even more interested in becoming an AF officer.	○	○	○	○	○	○	●	○
If the AF had provided an opportunity for learning a foreign language while I was in college (such as a summer abroad program), I would have been even more interested in becoming an AF officer.	○	○	○	○	○	○	●	○
I would have been willing to spend an extra year in college to learn a foreign language if the Air Force paid for it.	○	○	○	○	○	○	●	○
I would have been discouraged from becoming an AF officer if I had to be proficient in a foreign language to qualify.	○	○	●	○	○	○	○	○
If I had been required to study a foreign language to become an AF officer, I would have been less interested in joining the AF.	○	○	●	○	○	○	○	○
I would have been willing to study a foreign language in college ONLY if it was Spanish, French, or German.	●	○	○	○	○	○	○	○
I wish there had been more time for me to study a foreign language in college.	○	○	○	○	○	○	●	○
Learning a foreign language would have kept me from focusing on my major or other classes.	○	○	○	●	○	○	○	○

<<Back | Exit | Next>>

Language Courses at ROTC Detachments

In fiscal year (FY) 2009, 144 detachments, including about 1,000 crosstown schools, produced 1,894 commissioned officers. Since language courses in college offer an important opportunity for officer candidates to acquire language proficiency, particularly in the short term, we researched the language offerings at a sample of 50 colleges and universities that host ROTC detachments. This small sample of schools included a variety of school types in terms of numbers of degrees awarded, numbers of commissions, and geographical distribution. We used the sampled schools' online course catalogs to determine which languages they offered and how many courses were available in each language. We counted only courses taught in the language and excluded courses using literature translated into English and courses that appeared not to focus primarily on teaching the language in question, such as cinema.

Sixty-three different languages were taught across the 50 schools, with a median of ten languages per school. Spanish, French, and German were taught everywhere except Embry Riddle, Florida, which offered only one language.[1] This is particularly noteworthy, given that in FY 2009 Embry Riddle commissioned 38 officers, the most of any detachment. Somewhat less common languages in the 50 schools were Chinese, Japanese, and Russian, followed by Italian, Arabic, Portuguese, Ancient Greek, Hebrew, and Korean. Beyond these were a large variety of European, Far Eastern, and African languages. Even Native American languages were represented. The number of languages offered tended to be related to the size of the schools; however, there were exceptions. For example, among the 50 colleges we looked at, the University of California, Los Angeles (UCLA) and Ohio State had the most, with 41 and 37 different languages taught, while Cornell University, which is half the size of UCLA, was third with 36 languages.

A median of 20, 18, and 13 courses were offered in Spanish, French, and German, respectively. All but eight schools offered at least eight courses in all three languages. Table E.1 shows the 12 most common languages, along with the median and the 10th percentile number of courses offered across the schools in each language. Most colleges offer at least four courses in these languages, although sometimes there are only two.[2]

The data show that ROTC cadets have reasonable opportunities to study foreign languages in college. The types of languages are, however, predictable, and many of the ROTC schools do not offer key strategic languages (such as Arabic and Urdu). Moreover, the total

---

[1] Mandarin was offered as part of the Asian Studies program.

[2] The table does not indicate the largest number of courses taught at any of the 50 schools because these can be quite large when compared to the majority of schools. If our reading of catalogs is correct, the University of Virginia, Main Campus, and Ohio State have by far the largest numbers of courses for these languages.

Table E.1
Most Commonly Offered Languages

Language	Number of Schools	Number of Courses in the Language	
		Median	10th percentile
Spanish	49	20	8
French	49	18	4
German	48	13	5
Japanese	40	9	4
Chinese	39	8	4
Russian	34	9	4
Italian	28	8	4
Arabic	27	6	4
Portuguese	23	9	2
Ancient Greek	20	7	3
Hebrew	20	6	2
Korean	16	8	2

number of courses in a particular language varies from school to school and from language to language, suggesting that students would not have comparable opportunities to learn at all schools or across languages within schools.

Additional Details on "Other" and Open-Ended Responses

Chapter Four summarizes the responses to the open-ended questions. This appendix provides the detail on which that summary was based. Tables F.1 through F.8 expand on several rows in Table 4.8 in Chapter Four (note that some rows in Table 4.8 are not displayed in greater detail in the appendix) and Tables F.9 through F.12 are elaborations of the themes on the "additional comments" item summarized in Table 4.9.

Each table from F.1 through F.8 represents the results for the eight "other (please specify)" items on the survey. Tables F.9 through F.12 show the individual categories within the major themes on the "additional comments" item that we summarized in Chapter Four.

For all tables, the number column shows how many respondents wrote something that fell within a given category. The percentages represent individuals whose responses are in the category out of the total number of people who wrote a response for the question. For Tables F.1 through F.8, that number is shown below the table. For Tables F.9 through F.12, that number is 1,151. The weighted percentages (explained in Chapter Four) can be interpreted as representing the proportion of Air Force officers who would have made a given type of comment had we used a random sample of officers.

Table F.1
Incentives: Other Benefits, Advantages, and Rewards Associated with Learning Languages

Category	Description	Example Write-In Response	Number	Percentage Unweighted	Percentage Weighted
Preference	Preferred duty assignment, location, or deployment opportunity	Opportunities for deployments to countries that speak the language. Opportunities to meet with foreign representatives or visitors.	100	24.63	23.82
Immersion	Opportunity for TDY, exchange program, or other travel opportunities	The ability to go TDY for a significant amount of time (2 weeks+) to a location where my language is spoken to refresh and practice my language skills on a regular basis.	93	22.91	21.79
Time	Sponsored time to learn foreign language during work time such as attending DLI or while in other full-time training (e.g., Squadron Officer School)	Time off to pursue language studies and a release from work requirements.	49	12.07	20.53
Utilization	Opportunity to use foreign-language skills for job or other mission duties	I want to know that I will get to use the language after putting all that work into it. If the Air Force wants me to learn a language, I would expect them to employ me in a situation where that training would be used. But right now, I believe that my language training has been useless.	64	15.76	15.09
Cross training	Cross training for a specific job opportunity, such as Regional Affairs Specialist (RAS), Attaché, or embassy assignment	A reasonable chance to pursue career opportunities to work in a mil group or as an attaché.	40	9.85	12.98
Financial	Foreign-language proficiency pay or bonus, special pay, bonus, or additional retirement options	If I actually got foreign-language proficiency pay in the first place. I passed the DLPT in Russian and can't get paid because it is a dominant in the services language list yet the CSAF [Chief of Staff of the Air Force] puts it as an immediate investment language. I don't get it.	51	12.56	9.14
Interpersonal communication	Increased ability to communicate with others	Be able to communicate with foreign military members.	24	5.91	6.23

Table F.1—Continued

Category	Description	Example Write-In Response	Number	Percentage Unweighted	Percentage Weighted
Valued by Air Force	Removal of disincentives such as being penalized or punished in career field for following different career path	Opportunities to live and work abroad without sacrificing opportunity for advancement within my primary career field.	13	3.20	4.98
Promotion and advancement	Requirement or points contributing toward promotion or other opportunities for advancement	Part of the officer promotion boards to Lt Col.	23	5.67	4.25
Recognition	Formal recognition shown through awards or titles, such as ribbons, medals, or special job titles	Awards or decorations for language proficiency.	20	4.93	2.23
Other	Not clearly represented by previous categories	My significant other also learned the language.	55	13.55	10.93

NOTE: There were a total of 406 comments, but the number column may sum to more than that because individuals sometimes offered comments spanning more than one category.

Table F.2
Disincentives: Other Concerns Associated with Learning Languages

Category	Description	Example Write-In Response	Number	Percentage Unweighted	Percentage Weighted
Resources	Language requirement may put a strain on limited resources	There are enough demands on personal time already with correspondence PME [professional military education] and long work hours. The AF is too busy doing more w/less to actually introduce a structured language-learning program without placing higher demands on off-duty time.	72	36.55	43.81
Utilization	Language is not currently being used or is not likely to be used in the future	Put in the effort for learning the language and then not being able to use it.	36	18.27	13.28
Undervalued	The Air Force doesn't value foreign-language capabilities	As is quite typical, the Air Force does not consider the value of its members' speaking a foreign language. Yes, the foreign-language proficiency pay is very good. But my impression is that Air Force leaders do not care about foreign languages nearly as much as the leaders of the Army and Navy.	30	15.23	16.47
Utility	Not all Air Force specialties need to have a language or that learning a language will not benefit careers, Air Force, or the mission	Foreign language should be left to the AFS that use it. Let us do the jobs we volunteered for. Ops tempo is high enough.	21	10.66	17.17
Promotion requirement	Language proficiency would be used to determine promotions	Concern that failure to gain a certain proficiency despite best, good faith efforts would adversely impact career opportunities and become a discriminator to a promotion board.	13	6.60	15.47
Attrition	Difficulty maintaining language skills	Difficulty maintaining newly gained language skills if not assigned to duty in a location that provides the opportunity to use the language skill.	12	6.09	10.82

Table F.2—Continued

Category	Description	Example Write-In Response	Number	Percentage Unweighted	Percentage Weighted
Difficulty learning	Learning a language or others being more skilled at learning a language; may also indicate concern about difficulty learning language with limited resources available (e.g., solely computer-based programs)	Not being given assignments, advancement, recognition or promotion opportunities because I'm not skilled or have great difficulty in learning languages while some [of] my contemporaries and colleagues are given better choice or preference of assignments or given more opportunities for advancement, recognition or promotions because they happen to be better at learning and developing language skills. We shouldn't be punished (purposely or inadvertently) later in our careers for not having language skills or having great difficulty in developing language skills when those skills were not entry requirements in the Air Force or through our commissioning sources nor are they currently considered core skills in most Air Force specialties.	15	7.61	8.20
		I am not concerned about learning another language. The real issue is being forced to learn a certain language I'm not interested in.	20	10.15	4.90

NOTE: There were a total of 197 comments, but the number column may sum to more than that because individuals sometimes offered comments spanning more than one category.

Table F.3
Other Reasons for How and Why They Learned the Language

Category	Description	Example Write-In Response	Number	Percentage Unweighted	Percentage Weighted
Immersion	Traveling to or living in country where language is spoken by natives	Lived in (only visited France) these countries and had to learn to get around, without formal language education.	174	38.84	37.10
Self-study	Self-study materials (e.g., Rosetta Stone, DVDs, study manuals)	Rosetta Stone classes as part of Air War College.	96	21.43	25.45
Job or community	Living or working in a job with foreign speakers	Picked up some Spanish by talking to coworkers when I worked in the food industry.	57	12.72	15.90
Education	Formal training and education programs (e.g., AF sponsored training, formal education)	On base classes in Korea and Japan.	98	21.43	12.82
Family and friends	Family members, relatives, spouse, or friends	Russian-speaking spouse.	59	13.17	10.81
Church	Mission-related training and work	Missionary Training Center.	76	16.96	9.57
Media	Popular media (e.g., watching TV, reading newspapers, magazines, novels, listening to radio)	I read Vietnamese books regularly to maintain and improve my proficiency.	28	6.25	7.28
Martial arts	Participation in karate or other martial arts training	Kempo Karate and CHA-3 Karate.	7	1.56	2.68
Extended immersion	Living in country as a child for an extended period or considers language to be primary language	Grew up as the son of a missionary in French West Africa from age 6–18.	14	3.13	2.50
Similarity of languages	Because it is very similar to another language in which respondent has proficiency	... is very similar to Dutch and therefore I can understand, speak, and read a great deal of the language based purely on my mastery of the Dutch/Flemish language.	6	1.34	0.77
Other	Not clearly represented by previous categories	Now I practice by using a combination of Chinese and English with my mom. I did not learn it from her growing up.	4	0.89	1.20

NOTE: There were a total of 448 comments, but the number column may sum to more than 448 because individuals sometimes offered comments spanning more than one category.

Table F.4
Other Types of Language-Related Courses in College

Category	Description	Example Write-In Response	Number	Percentage Unweighted	Percentage Weighted
Language-focused	Speech, linguistics, translation, or communication of language	Phonetics, linguistics, and grammar.	61	29.61	31.52
World affairs	Culture, history, political science, government, or relations	Current events in Latin America.	59	28.64	23.92
Immersion	Respondent participated in study abroad or all courses were taught in language	I did a study abroad program in Berlin.	37	17.96	14.20
Business	Course focused on business concepts (e.g., business and economic courses for specific language)	Economics of Russia.	22	10.68	7.08
Technical language	Course(s) taught for specific discipline incorporating technical language (e.g., science, engineering, medical)	Aeronautical engineering in French at USAFA.	18	8.74	16.95
Test or credit	Respondent participated in College Level Examination Program (CLEP) or placed out of language requirement	I CLEP'ed 16 credit hours or 5 semesters of Portuguese due to in country experience learning the language.	14	6.80	5.50
Literature	Literature, reading, or novels	Poetry.	12	5.83	4.94
Language-focused subset	Course on translation	I also took a course in Spanish-English Translation.	10	4.85	3.23
Language-focused subset	Course on specific linguistics or phonetics	Phonetics.	10	4.85	2.97
Research	Course was for independent study, thesis, or independent research	Independent study on Puerto Rico.	10	4.85	2.78
Unsure	Respondent didn't remember or was uncertain of responses provided	I am only going from memory. I do not have my transcript in front of me.	7	3.40	1.62
Other	Not clearly represented by previous categories	I earned credits serving as a Chinese tutor.	17	8.25	9.50

NOTE: There were a total of 206 comments, but the number column may sum to more than 206 because individuals sometimes offered comments spanning more than one category.

Table F.5
Other Reasons for Taking This Language in High School

Category	Description	Example Write-In Response	Number	Percentage Unweighted	Percentage Weighted
Prerequisite	To be eligible or competitive for a program or for college admission.	Required for college admission.	20	27.03	32.99
Personal development	To satisfy an interest or to maintain or improve language skills	I thought it was a good skill to have and good for future relations as few Americans are bilingual but many Europeans can speak multiple languages.	9	12.16	22.16
Requirement	To fulfill a requirement (e.g., graduation, scholarship requirement)	Requirement to graduate.	12	16.22	21.49
Community	To communicate with others in hometown or local community	I grew up in Texas. . . . You can't supervise any minimum wage workers if you don't speak Spanish.	12	16.22	11.26
Heritage and background	One or more family members is a foreign national, language is respondent's native language, or respondent grew up in foreign country	My family has a French background, so I took the class for heritage reasons.	12	16.22	7.01
Travel	To study abroad, travel, or to live; may also have taken classes while immersed in country	I was living in Austria, and wanted to further my knowledge of German, while simultaneously not losing the German I had learned up to that point.	5	6.76	4.93
External influence	Because parents or advisors recommended or required it	My parents made me.	3	4.05	1.29
Easy	To raise GPA or because it was easy; may have also taken language because of previous knowledge of language which aided in testing out of further requirements	Took Spanish, as it is similar to Italian, which was spoken in the household I grew up in during my early childhood.	2	2.70	0.66
Other	Not clearly represented by previous categories	I wish now I thought language skills were important when I was in high school. It would have been much better to learn the different languages earlier in life.	7	9.46	3.31

NOTE: There were a total of 74 comments, but the number column may sum to more than 74 because individuals sometimes offered comments spanning more than one category.

Table F.6
Other Ways They Maintained Their Language Skills Since College (High School)

| | | | Percentage | |
Category	Description	Example Write-In Response	Number	Unweighted	Weighted
Travel	Traveling to foreign countries, living abroad, or TDYs to country	Various TDYs to Germany while stationed at RAF Lakenheath early in my career.	56 (16)	19.31 (22.54)	26.98 (10.73)
Reading	Reading newspapers or books, browsing the web, and reading news online	Read French news on the internet.	100 (16)	34.48 (22.54)	20.89 (36.52)
Media	Watching TV, news, or movies; may also listen to the radio, podcasts, or music	Watched movies in the language.	72 (15)	24.83 (21.13)	17.72 (8.80)
Minimal maintenance	Respondent has engaged in few to no activities to maintain language skills	Minimal time keeping up with the proficiency.	35 (13)	12.07 (18.31)	12.80 (16.70)
Communication	Talking with non-foreign national family members in residence; may also use foreign language to talk with relatives, coworkers, or others in community	Lived/Worked in California and living/working in Texas exposed me to the Spanish language.	39 (9)	13.45 (12.68)	11.06 (15.90)
Close contact with native speaker(s)	Communicating frequently with family member(s) who are native speakers; may also be the respondent's native language	My wife's family only speak Spanish (Mexican).	25 (12)	8.62 (16.90)	9.52 (5.17)
Self-study	Using self-guided study techniques (e.g., CDs, tapes, Rosetta Stone, or textbooks)	I continue to use my tapes, CDs and Rosetta Stone to work on the languages, as time permits.	21 (4)	7.24 (5.63)	6.37 (6.22)
Translation	Translating	I continue to do freelance translations in Russian-English.	6 (0)	2.07 (0.00)	5.75 (0.00)
Education	Teaching, tutoring, or assisting with language development; may also have maintained language by enrolling in schools or classes as a student	Spent two months taking classes twice a week at the language center in town.	14 (6)	4.83 (8.45)	3.48 (15.07)
Church activities	Through engagement in bible study, mission work, or other church-related work	Weekly biblical study.	8 (1)	2.76 (1.41)	2.56 (0.84)
Other	Not clearly represented by previous categories	To show off.	6	2.07 (2.82)	4.08 (0.77)

NOTE: Numbers in parentheses refer to responses to high school. Numbers not in parentheses refer to responses about college. Total comments = 290 (71). The number column may sum to more than 290 (71) because individuals sometimes offered comments spanning more than one category.

Table F.7
Other DLI Training They Received

Category	Description	Example Write-In Response	Number	Percentage Unweighted	Percentage Weighted
Other course	Language training provided as part of another training course	Received it while at Air Advisors Training.	26	34.21	43.16
DLI instructors	Language training provided by DLI instructors	DLI instructor taught intro class at our unit for personnel deploying to Afghanistan.	20	26.32	28.27
Self-guided	Respondent engaged in self-guided language development activities	Spanish language cassettes.	19	25.00	25.61
Specific program	Attended a specific language training program	DLI East, AFPAK Hands Program (with DLS).	4	5.26	1.44
Other	Not clearly represented by previous categories	Not sure what DLI is…but I did a one-month Cadet Summer Research Program in France in college.	8	10.53	2.86

NOTE: There were a total of 76 comments, but the number column may sum to more than 76 because individuals sometimes offered comments spanning more than one category.

Table F.8
Other Language-Related Military Training They Received

Category	Description	Example Write-In Response	Number	Percentage Unweighted	Percentage Weighted
Formal education	Language training provided as part of formal education	Part of USMC Command & Staff College.	17	32.69	33.05
Immersion	Language skills were developed during immersion program or immersion experience	1.5 week TDY to Argentina.	18	34.62	26.23
Deployment training	Language training was provided as part of instruction prior to deployment	Classroom training prior to deployment.	4	7.69	21.92
Tutoring	Provided by tutor or on an individual basis	One on one tutoring provided at the military job location.	7	13.46	10.44
Self-guided	Provided through self-guided activities	Podcast/vodcast.	6	11.54	7.52

NOTE: There were a total of 52 comments, but the number column may sum to more than 52 because individuals sometimes offered comments spanning more than one category.

Table F.9
General Open-Ended Comments: Positive Comments Theme

Category	Description	Example Write-In Response	Number	Percentage Unweighted	Percentage Weighted
General support	General positive support for language development or willingness to learn a language	I also liked that it, let me express my desire, is not in the pay but in the skills and doors that open with knowing languages and cultures.	221	19.20	24.12
Mission success	Language skills are beneficial to performing job duties, achieving mission success, or in building foreign relations	I feel that learning foreign languages is a very important mission for the USAF. With our NATO partners and the rest of the world learning and demonstrating proficiency in English, I think it's critical for the United States to develop and maintain at the very least a cadre of officers and enlisted personnel skilled in foreign languages to demonstrate to our allies that we care. Furthermore, the cultural education required to attain a higher level of language proficiency develops in a person an awareness of different ways of doing things in other parts of the world—this awareness, if present in a greater proportion of our officers, would greatly help us to sidestep the sort of grievous faux pas we've been committing on a rather grand scale in our overseas operations (I believe).	126	10.95	9.35
Language-career	Respondent has duties that specifically utilize language skills (e.g., RAS); may also perceive importance to future duties within the AF or in civilian sector	I am very interested in becoming a foreign area officer, air attaché or political/military affairs officer. I would welcome any opportunity to study a language in an in-residence program.	42	3.65	1.64
Personal background	Respondent has family background or affinity for languages	I grew up in a family where foreign languages were important. My father speaks two foreign languages and at age 65 started taking a third because my brother married someone speaking the language and he wanted to be able to speak to her family. My stepmother is European and speaks two languages other than English and understands some of two more. Growing up we had friends of all nationalities and were encouraged to learn about their cultures. I hope to instill this love of languages and other cultures in my children, as I know it makes it easier to understand why people do the things they do.	29	2.52	1.61

NOTE: Individuals sometimes offered comments spanning more than one category.

Table F.10
General Open-Ended Comments: Potential Barriers Theme

Category	Description	Example Write-In Response	Number	Percentage Unweighted	Percentage Weighted
Time	Time was a barrier to developing and retaining language skills	When I returned to Japan as a Major, I was really starting over and didn't have the time to put into learning Japanese during my assignment. That was unfortunate.	257	22.33	35.47
Utilization	Concerns that language skills would not be fully utilized in the AF	Another worthless requirement that will be leveled on officers. People fill these to fill a square. There is NO value added if it is square filling. If a job requires language skills then send them to class to learn the language then to the job. Don't add another WORTHLESS SQUARE to the long list of WORTHLESS SQUARES we already have!!!!!!!!!!	316	27.45	24.28
Role overload	Subcategory of "Time" and reflects concerns of adding requirements to current heavy workload or existing personal obligations (e.g., family)	I am interested in getting my proficiency back up, but with my job (50–60 hrs/wk) and family commitments (5 kids), there just isn't any time for me to do so.	169	14.68	21.90
Career field	Subcategory of "Utilization" and indicates a lack of opportunities to learn or use languages in career field; may include comments that AF should match personnel interests and backgrounds to assignments or educational opportunities	My career field will not allow me to pursue IAS International Affairs Specialist] opportunities although I have extensive foreign-language training and cultural knowledge.	265	23.02	19.81
Incentives	Subcategory of "AF Support" and reflects specific concerns about incentives to learn and retain language skills	The AF should value and desire people to learn a foreign language, but if they want people to learn one, pay for it.	201	17.46	15.51
AF support	Concern that the AF is not doing enough to promote foreign languages	I think the Air Force is severely behind in giving its officers the time and ability to learn about other cultures and get language training.	213	18.51	15.09
Language requirements	Opposes language requirements for either accession or promotion	I find foreign language invaluable on a personal and social level, but requiring proficiency for officers would probably lose some great people whose strengths lie elsewhere. Because the USAF doesn't provide realistic immersion or career opportunities to most airmen who desire to learn or maintain language skills, forcing an entry or promotion language requirement upon those who don't desire or have the aptitude to learn a language is misplaced.	130	11.29	14.23

Table F.10—Continued

Category	Description	Example Write-In Response	Number	Percentage Unweighted	Percentage Weighted
College commitment	Subcategory of "Time" and indicates respondent would have found it difficult to learn language in college	I was very interested in learning Arabic at USAFA but the heavy concentration on an engineering general-education curriculum was distracting and hard to switch gears during the days and weekends of studying—from pure mathematics and engineering concepts to memorizing vocabulary and associating with images, etc.	48	4.17	5.91
Career progression	Concern that taking time away from career field for language would be detrimental to career path	I think learning foreign languages is an important skill for Air Force officers but I am hesitant to actively pursue the language because I think that it puts you on a path that takes you away from your AFSC and makes it difficult to return. If there were language training opportunities or chances to do a tour where language skills were required, but then be able to return to your previous career path without being penalized or pigeonholed, I think more officers would be inclined to put greater emphasis on learning and maintaining languages.	43	3.74	2.45
Proficiency test	Concerns that the language proficiency tests are not valid	There is also the subject of the testing. Many language tests have been recalled/revised because of test errors and the quality of the audio is questionable as well. The DLPT IV was an outdated test and needed to be replaced, however, the DLPT V is a disaster that the DoD should stop trying to justify and start trying to fix.	20	1.74	0.61

NOTE: Individuals sometimes offered comments spanning more than one category.

Table F.11
General Open-Ended Comments: Implementation Theme

Category	Description	Example Write-In Response	Number	Percentage Unweighted	Percentage Weighted
Immersion and retention	Importance of immersion for developing and retaining language skills; comment may also indicate language attrition	I really enjoyed Spanish for the 6 years I took it in High School. By the end [of] my last AP course, I was somewhat fluent. I just needed an immersion to really solidify things. It's been 10 years since then and I now just have remnants of my Spanish. I would love the opportunity to learn it again.	194	16.85	15.88
Specificity	Should limit support of language for specific career fields or languages (e.g., strategic languages), or to mission specific training (e.g., prior to deployment).	Certain career fields like Acquisition do not need expanded language skills; if required then can send Officers to specific language courses prior to overseas assignments.	63	5.47	7.63
Early education	Importance of developing language skills early in one's life or early in one's career	If not immersed in environment during fundamental development stages of life, i.e., 7–12 years of age, cultural fluency is unattainable on comprehensive cognitive level.	63	5.47	5.56
Information	Additional information regarding language programs and resources	I would appreciate the opportunity to learn or improve my language skills, but as an already commissioned officer I have never been told of any possibilities.	49	4.26	2.62
Identification of personnel	Support for early career or testing to identify those who have proficiency in a language or have the ability to learn languages	Have DLAB be required test. Through my career I have come across several officers who spoke critical languages like Dari and Mandarin and they were in personnel or some other field where they wouldn't use them. Also, in one case they didn't want to tell the Air Force so they wouldn't be deployed or used in that capacity.	5	0.43	0.20

NOTE: Individuals sometimes offered comments spanning more than one category.

Table F.12
General Open-Ended Comments: Resources and Programs Theme

Category	Description	Example Write-In Response	Number	Percentage Unweighted	Percentage Weighted
Resources	Desire to have access to programs or resources	The foreign area officer program in the AF does not seem to be widely available and is not well known in the line AF. It seems an emphasis is needed in both of these areas in order for the AF to really push language learning.	267	23.20	18.46
Rosetta Stone	Mentions Rosetta Stone	I have spent time using items like Rosetta Stone to help me learn a little Arabic when I was stationed in Egypt, and French while stationed in Belgium.	93	8.08	8.33
Rosetta Stone—positive	Positive support for Rosetta Stone	The military's access to free Rosetta Stone is an amazing resource.	20	1.74	1.93
Rosetta Stone access	Desire to have access to Rosetta Stone	The Rosetta Stone program is good, but it should be readily available in any location. I couldn't get a subscription (for Arabic) through the military when I was deployed in Iraq.	29	2.52	2.60
Rosetta Stone—negative	Negative experience with Rosetta Stone	I have experienced learning a language from Rosetta Stone, DLI, and through immersion. From first hand experience, Rosetta Stone is a waste of government money. No computer based system or structured course can teach you the slang and differences in the language from the textbook language.	27	2.35	2.47
DLI	Mentions DLI	I just wish there were more opportunities out there for AF Officers to become proficient in other languages (i.e., Defense Language School in CA).	84	7.30	5.31
DLI—positive	Positive support for DLI	Based on my experience as a full-time DLI French student, full-time and immersion training is the most optimal and effective means of learning a language.	11	0.96	0.33
DLI—access	Desire to attend DLI	I think the AF should send anyone and everyone who is interested to DLI to learn an AF mission critical language. I am still trying to get sent to DLI to learn Turkish.	36	3.13	2.38

Table F.12—Continued

Category	Description	Example Write-In Response	Number	Percentage Unweighted	Percentage Weighted
DLI—negative	Negative experience with DLI	My experience in DLI-W was good, but the contracted company (Dari) did not have very qualified instructors on hand. My first instructor was a native speaker and was also [a] well experienced language educator. The second instructor was a medical doctor by training (native speaker), but could not teach beginning students. The third instructor was a medical doctor also, but better suited to teaching beginning students. All-in-all they were not prepared to handle the loss of the first instructor and the result was a serious loss of proficiency while I was being belittled by the second instructor.	6	0.52	0.23
Language Air Studies Immersion (LASI) program	Mentions LASI program	I was able to participate in both LASI (one month immersion in Italy) and one-on-one Italian tutoring (100 hours in DC) funded by the AF.	21	1.82	0.52

Note: Individuals sometimes offered comments spanning more than one category.

References

ACTFL—*See* American Council on the Teaching of Foreign Languages.

Air Force Instruction 16-109, *Operations Support: International Affairs Specialist (IAS) Program*, September 3, 2010.

American Council on the Teaching of Foreign Languages, "ACTFL Proficiency Guidelines C Speaking," 1999. As of February 15, 2012:
http://www.actfl.org/files/public/Guidelinesspeak.pdf

Arizona State University, Admission, web page, 2010. As of February 3, 2012:
http://www.students.asu.edu/admission

———, Chinese Language Flagship Program, web page, 2012. As of February 6, 2012:
http://chineseflagship.asu.edu/

———, Chinese Language Flagship Program, ASU Domestic Study, Flagship Course Descriptions, 2012. As of April 25, 2012:
http://chineseflagship.asu.edu/curriculum/course-descriptions

Aud, Susan, William Hussar, Michael Planty, Thomas Snyder, Kevin Bianco, Mary Ann Fox, Lauren Frohlich, Jana Kemp, and Lauren Drake, *The Condition of Education 2010*, Washington, D.C.: National Center for Education Statistics, Institute of Education Sciences, U.S. Department of Education, June 2010. As of February 15, 2012:
http://nces.ed.gov/pubsearch/pubsinfo.asp?pubid=2010028

Bandura, Albert, *Self-Efficacy: The Exercise of Control*, New York: Freeman, 1997.

Barrick, Murray R., and Michael K. Mount, "The Big Five Personality Dimensions and Job Performance: A Meta-Analysis," *Personnel Psychology*, No. 44, Spring 1991, pp. 1–26.

Bermel, Neil, and Kagan, Olga, "The Maintenance of Written Russian in Heritage Speakers," in Olga Kagan and Benjamin Rifkin, eds., *The Learning and Teaching of Slavic Languages and Cultures*, Bloomington, Ind.: Slavica Pub, 2000.

Brecht, Richard D., E. Golonka, K. Müller, W. Rivers, and J. P. Robinson, "An Introduction to America's Language Needs and Resources," presented at the National Language Conference, University of Maryland, June 22–24, 2004. As of February 3, 2012:
http://www.casl.umd.edu/node/1748

Brigham Young University, Admissions, web page, undated. As of February 3, 2012:
http://saas.byu.edu/tools/b4byu/sites/b4/

———, Chinese Flagship Center, web page, undated. As of February 3, 2012:
http://chineseflagship.byu.edu/chineseflagship/index.html

Bryn Mawr College, The Russian Language Flagship, web page, 2012. As of February 3, 2012:
http://www.brynmawr.edu/russian/flagship.htm

———, Undegraduate Admission & Financial Aid, web page, 2012. As of February 3, 2012:
http://www.brynmawr.edu/admissions

Burke, Lisa A., and Holly M. Hutchins, "Training Transfer: An Integrative Literature Review," *Human Resource Development Review,* Vol. 6, No. 3, September 2007, pp. 263–296.

Carroll, John B., "Twenty-Five Years of Research on Foreign Language Aptitude," in Karl Conrad Diller, ed., *Individual Differences and Universals in Language Learning Aptitude,* Rowley, Mass.: Newbury House, 1981, pp. 83–118.

Carroll, John B., and Stanley Sapon, *The Modern Language Aptitude Test—Form A,* New York: The Psychological Corporation, 1958.

Chairman of the Joint Chiefs of Staff Instruction 3126.01, *Language and Regional Expertise Planning,* November 27, 2010. As of April 5, 2011:
http://www.dtic.mil/cjcs_directives/cdata/unlimit/3126_01.pdf

Chiswick, Barry R., and Paul W. Miller, "The Critical Period Hypothesis for Language Learning: What the 2000 U.S. Census Says," Bonn, Germany: The Institute for the Study of Labor (IZA), 2007.

Clark, J. L. D., "Language," in T. S. Barrows et al., eds., *College Students' Knowledge and Beliefs: A Survey of Global Understanding,* New Rochelle, N.Y.: Change Magazine Press, 1981.

Conway, John L., "The View from the Tower of Babel: Air Force Foreign Language Posture for Global Engagement," *Air & Space Power Journal,* Summer 2005, pp. 57–69.

———, "Civilian Language Education in America How the Air Force and Academia Can Thrive Together," *Air & Space Power Journal,* Fall 2010, pp. 74–88.

Corin, A., "A Course to Convert Czech Proficiency to Proficiency in Croatian and Serbian," in S. B. Stryker and B. L. Leaver, eds., *Content-Based Instruction in Foreign-Language Education: Models and Methods,* Washington, D.C.: Georgetown University Press, 1997, pp. 78–106.

Cummins, Jim, "Bilingual and Immersion Programs," in Michael H. Long and Catherine J. Doughty, eds., *The Handbook of Language Teaching,* New York: Wiley-Blackwell, 2009, Ch. 10.

Davidson, Dan E. and Susan Goodrich Lehmann, "A Longitudinal Survey of the Language Learning Careers of ACTR Advanced Students of Russian: 1976–2000," *Russian Language Journal,* Vol. 55, 2001–2005, pp. 193–221.

Deci, Edward L., and Richard M. Ryan, *Intrinsic Motivation and Self-Determination in Human Behavior,* New York: Plenum, 1985.

Defense Language Institute Foreign Language Center, Defense Language Proficiency Test (DLPT) Program, Presidio of Monterey, Calif., July 10, 2009. As of August 30, 2010:
http://www.dliflc.edu/archive/documents/DLPT_Credit_by_Exam_Policy.pdf

———, Catalog 2009–2010, Presidio of Monterey, Calif., July 27, 2010. As of August 30, 2010:
http://www.dliflc.edu/publications.aspx

Department of Defense Directive 3000.05, *Military Support for Stability, Security, Transition, and Reconstruction (SSTR) Operations,* November 28, 2005.

Department of Defense Directive 5160.41E, "Defense Language Program (DLP)," change 1, Washington, D.C.: Under Secretary of Defense for Personnel and Readiness, May 27, 2010.

Department of Defense Instruction 5160.70, *Management of DoD Language and Regional Proficiency Capabilities,* Washington, D.C.: Under Secretary of Defense for Personnel and Readiness, June 12, 2007.

——— 7280.03, *Foreign Language Proficiency Bonus,* August 20, 2007.

DeKeyser, Robert M., "The Robustness of Critical Period Effects in Second Language Acquisition," *Studies in Second Language Acquisition,* Vol. 22, 2000, pp. 499–533.

DeKeyser, Robert, and Jenifer Larson-Hall, "What Does the Critical Period Really Mean?" in Judith F. Kroll and Annette M. B. De Groot, eds., *Handbook of Bilingualism: Psycholinguistic Approaches,* Oxford: Oxford University Press, 2005.

Dewaele, Jean-Marc, and Adrian Furnham, "Extraversion: The Unloved Variable in Applied Linguistic Research," *Language Learning,* Vol. 49, No. 3, 1999, pp. 509–544.

DLIFLC—*See* Defense Language Institute Foreign Language Center.

DoD—*See* U.S. Department of Defense.

Dörnyei, Zoltán, "On the Teachability of Communication Strategies," *TESOL Quarterly*, Vol. 29, No. 1, Spring 1995, pp. 55–85.

———, "Attitudes, Orientations, and Motivations in Language Learning: Advances in Theory, Research, and Applications," *Language Learning*, Vol. 53, No. 1, 2003, pp. 3–32.

———, "Individual Differences in Second Language Acquisition," *AILA Review*, Vol. 19, 2006, pp. 42–68.

Dörnyei, Zoltán, and Richard Schmidt, eds. *Motivation and Second Language Acquisition*, Honolulu: Second Language Teaching and Curriculum Center, 2001.

Ehrman, Madeline, "The Learning Alliance: Conscious and Unconscious Aspects of the Second Language Teacher's Role," *System*, Vol. 26, No. 1, March 1998, pp. 93–106.

———, "Personality and Good Language Learners," in Carol Griffiths, ed., *Lessons from Good Language Learners*, Cambridge, Mass.: Cambridge University Press, 2008, pp. 61–72.

Ehrman, Madeline E., Betty Lou Leaver, and Rebecca L. Oxford, "A Brief Overview of Individual Differences in Second Language Learning," *System*, Vol. 31, No. 3, September 2003, pp. 313–330.

Ellis, Rod, "Principles of Instructed Second Language Acquisition," CAL Digest Series, Washington, D.C.: Center for Applied Linguistics, December 2008.

European Commission, *Key Facts and Figures About Europe and the Europeans*, 2007. As of April 5, 2011: http://ec.europa.eu/publications/booklets/eu_glance/66/en.pdf

Foreign Service Institute, *Language Continuum*, Arlington, Va.: U.S. Department of State, undated. As of April 5, 2011: http://fsitraining.state.gov/training/Language%20Continuum.pdf

FSI—*See* Foreign Service Institute.

Gardner, Robert C., *Social Psychology and Second Language Learning: The Role of Attitudes and Motivation*, London: Edward Arnold, 1985.

———, "The Socio-Educational Model of Language Learning: Assumptions, Findings, and Issues," *Language Learning*, Vol. 38, No. 1, 1988, pp. 101–126.

Gardner, Robert C., and Wallace E. Lambert, *Attitudes and Motivation in Second-Language Learning*, Rowley, Mass.: Newbury House, 1972.

Gleason, Jean Berko, ed., *You Can Take It with You: Helping Students Maintain Foreign Language Skills Beyond the Classroom*, Language in Education: Theory and Practice 71, Washington, D.C.: Center for Applied Linguistics, 1988.

Goldberg, L. R., "An Alternative 'Description of Personality': The Big-Five Factor Structure," *Journal of Personality and Social Psychology*, Vol. 59, No. 6, December 1990, pp. 1216–1229.

Gor, Kira, and Karen Vatz, "Less Commonly Taught Languages: Issues in Learning and Teaching," in Michael H. Long and Catherine J. Doughty, eds., *The Handbook of Language Teaching*, Oxford: Wiley-Blackwell, 2009, pp. 234–249.

Griffiths, Carol, "Strategies and Good Language Learners," in Carol Griffiths, ed., *Lessons from Good Language Learners*, Cambridge, Mass.: Cambridge University Press, 2008, pp. 83–98.

Grigorenko, Elena L., Robert J. Sternberg, and Madeline E. Ehrman, "A Theory-Based Approach to the Measurement of Foreign Language Learning Ability: The CANAL-F Theory and Test," *Modern Language Journal*, Vol. 84, No. 3, 2000, pp. 390–405.

Grosjean, François, 2010, "Bilingualism's Best-Kept Secret: How Extensive It Is," *Psychology Today*, November 1, 2010. As of April 5, 2011: http://www.psychologytoday.com/blog/life-bilingual/201011/bilingualisms-best-kept-secret-how-extensive-it-is

Hakuta, Kenji, "A Critical Period for Second Language Acquisition?" in Donald B. Bailey, Jr., John T. Bruer, Frank Symons, and J. Lichtman, eds., *Critical Thinking About Critical Periods*, Baltimore, Md.: Brookes, 2001, pp. 192–205.

Hammill, Donald D., "On Defining Learning Disabilities: An Emerging Consensus," *Journal of Learning Disabilities*, Vol. 23, No. 2, 1990, pp. 74–84.

Harley, Birgit, and Doug Hart, "Language Aptitude and Second Language Proficiency in Classroom Learners of Different Starting Ages," *Studies in Second Language Acquisition*, Vol. 19, No. 3, September 1997, pp. 379–400.

Howard University, Admission, web page, undated. As of February 3, 2012: http://www.howard.edu/enrollment/admission

———, African Language Flagship, web page, undated. As of February 3, 2012: http://www.coas.howard.edu/languageflagship/

ILR—*See* Interagency Language Roundtable.

Indiana University, The Center for Chinese Language Pedagogy, web page, undated. As of February 3, 2012: https://www.indiana.edu/~cclp/main/

Indiana University, Office of Admissions, web page, 2011. As of February 3, 2012: http://www.indiana.edu/~iuadmit

Interagency Language Roundtable, "About the ILR," 2011a. As of April 5, 2011: http://www.govtilr.org/IRL%20History.htm

———, "History of the ILR Scale," 2011b. As of February 16, 2012: http://www.govtilr.org/Skills/IRL%20Scale%20History.htm

———, "Interagency Language Roundtable Language Skill Level Descriptions—Listening," 2011c. As of April 26, 2012: http://www.govtilr.org/Skills/ILRscale3.htm

———, "Interagency Language Roundtable Language Skill Level Descriptions—Reading," 2011d. As of April 26, 2012: http://www.govtilr.org/Skills/ILRscale4.htm

———, "Interagency Language Roundtable Language Skill Level Descriptions—Speaking," 2011e. As of April 26, 2012: http://www.govtilr.org/Skills/ILRscale2.htm

———, "Self-Assessment of Listening Proficiency," 2011f. As of February 16, 2012: http://www.govtilr.org/Publications/listenngsa.html

———, "Self-Assessment of Speaking Proficiency," 2011g. As of February 16, 2012: http://www.govtilr.org/Publications/speakingsa.html

———, "Self-Assessment of Reading Proficiency," 2011h. As of February 16, 2012: http://www.govtilr.org/Publications/readingsa.html

Jackson, Frederick H., and Marsha A. Kaplan, 2003, "Theory and Practice in Government Language Teaching," draft, 2007. As of April 5, 2011: http://www.govtilr.org/Publications/TESOL03ReadingFull.htm

Javad Riasati, M., and N. Noordin, "Antecedents of Willingness to Communicate: A Review of Literature," *Studies in Literature and Language*, Vol. 3, No. 2, 2011, pp. 74–80.

Jessner, Ulrike, "Metalinguistic Awareness in Multilinguals: Cognitive Aspects of Third Language Learning," *Language Awareness*, Vol. 8, No. 3–4, 1999, pp. 201–209.

Kagan, O., and Dillon, K., "Issues in Heritage Language Learning in the United States," in V. Deusen-Scholl and N. Hornberger, eds., *Encyclopedia of Language and Education*, Vol. 4: *Second and Foreign Language Education*, Springer, 2008, pp. 143–156.

Kavale, Kenneth A., "How Many Learning Disabilities Are There? A Commentary on Stanovich's 'Dysrationalia: A New Specific Learning Disability,'" *Journal of Learning Disabilities*, Vol. 26, No. 8, October 1993, pp. 520–523.

KewalRamani, Angelina, Lauren Gilbertson, Mary Ann Fox, and Stephen Provasnik, *Status and Trends in the Education of Racial and Ethnic Minorities*, Washington, D.C.: National Center for Education Statistics, Institute of Education Sciences, U.S. Department of Education, September 2007.

Klein, Elaine C., "Second Versus Third Language Acquisition: Is There a Difference?" *Language Learning*, Vol. 45, No. 3, September 1995, pp. 419–465.

Kroll, J., "Bilinguals and Second Language Learners: Juggling Two Languages in One Mind and One Brain," presented at Second Language Research Forum, College Park, Md.: October 14–17, 2010.

Lambert, Richard D., and Barbara F. Freed, eds., *The Loss of Language Skills*, Rowley, Mass.: Newbury House Publishers, 1982.

Language Flagship, "The Flagship History," 2012. As of April 5, 2011: http://www.thelanguageflagship.org/about-us/the-flagship-history

Lantolf, James P., and Steven L. Thorne, *Sociocultural Theory and the Genesis of Second Language Development*, Oxford University Press, 2006.

Leaver, Betty Lou, and Sabine Atwell, "Preliminary Qualitative Findings from a Study of the Processes Leading to the Advanced Professional Proficiency Level (ILR 4)," in Betty Lou Leaver and Boris Shekhtman, eds., *Developing Professional-Level Language Proficiency*, Cambridge, Mass.: Cambridge University Press, 2002, pp. 260–279.

Lenneberg, Eric H., "The Capacity for Language Acquisition," in Jerry A. Fodor, Jerrold J. Katz, Q. V. Quine, and Noam Chomsky, *The Structure of Language: Readings in the Philosophy of Language*, Englewood Cliffs, N.J.: Prentice-Hall, Inc., 1964.

———, *Biological Foundations of Language*, New York: Wiley, 1967.

Linck, J., S. Jackson, A. Bowles, S. Campbell, M. Mislevy, J. Koeth, C. Blake, R. Willis, R. Corbett, B. Smith, and M. Bunting, "What Characteristics of the Individual Are Needed to Predict Successful Post-Critical Period Language Learning?" paper presented at Second Language Research Forum 2010, College Park, Md., 2010.

Long, Michael H., and Catherine J. Doughty, eds., *The Handbook of Language Teaching*, New York: Wiley-Blackwell, 2009.

MacIntyre, P. D., and C. Charos, "Personality, Attitudes and Affect as Predictors of Second Language Communication," *Journal of Language and Social Psychology*, Vol. 15, No. 1, 1996, pp. 3–26.

McKeen, Gina V., "AF Officials Launch Language Program for Airmen," Air Force Personnel Center Public Affairs, April 8, 2010. As of January 19, 2010: http://www.afpc.af.mil/news/story.asp?id=123198875

Meara, Paul M., "LLAMA Language Aptitude Tests: The Manual," Swansea: Lognostics, 2005. As of February 15, 2012: http://www.lognostics.co.uk/tools/llama/llama_manual.pdf

Michigan State University, Arabic Language Flagship, web page, 2008. As of February 3, 2012: http://www.arabicflagship.msu.edu

———, Office of Admissions, web page, 2012. As of February 3, 2012: http://www.admissions.msu.edu

Montrul, Silvina, "Heritage Language Programs," in M. Long and C. Doughty, eds., *The Handbook of Language Teaching*, New York: Wiley-Blackwell, 2009.

National Security Education Program, website, undated. As of March 2, 2012: http://www.nsep.gov/about/mission/

Noels, K. A., "New Orientations in Language Learning Motivation: Towards a Model of Intrinsic, Extrinsic, and Integrative Orientations and Motivation," in Z. Dörnyei and R. Schmidt, eds., *Motivation and Second Language Acquisition*, Honolulu: University of Hawaii Press, 2001, pp. 43–68.

Noels, Kimberly A., Luc G. Pelletier, Richard Clement, and Robert J. Vallerand, "Why Are You Learning A Second Language? Motivational Orientations and Self-Determination Theory," *Language Learning*, Vol. 50, No. 1, March 2000, pp. 57–85.

NSEP—*See* National Security Education Program.

Ohio State University, Future Students, web page, 2012. As of February 3, 2012:
http://www.osu.edu/futurestudents

———, Midwest US–China Flagship Program, web page, 2010. As of February 3, 2012:
http://www.chineseflagship.osu.edu/

Oxford, Rebecca L., *Language Learning Strategies: What Every Teacher Should Know*, Boston: Heinle & Heinle, 1990.

Oyama, Susan, "The Sensitive Period and Comprehension of Speech," *NABE: The Journal for the National Association for Bilingual Education*, Vol. 3, No. 1, Fall 1978, pp. 25–39.

Peterson, C. R., and A. R. Al-Haik, "The Development of the Defense Language Aptitude Battery (DLAB)," *Educational and Psychological Measurement*, Vol. 36, 1976, pp. 369–380.

Pimsleur, P., *Pimsleur Language Aptitude Battery,* New York: Harcourt Brace Jovanovich, 1966.

Portland State University, College of Liberal Arts & Sciences: World Languages and Literatures, web page, undated. As of February 3, 2012:
http://www.pdx.edu/wll/

———, Enrollment Management & Student Affairs: Admissions, web page, 2012. As of February 3, 2012:
http://www.pdx.edu/admissions

Reed, D. J., and C. W. Stansfield, "The Use of the Modern Language Aptitude Test in the Assessment of Foreign Language Learning Disability—What's at Stake?" paper presented at the Language Testing Ethics Conference, Pasadena, California, May 16–18, 2002.

Rhodes, Nancy C., and Ingrid Pufahl, *Foreign Language Teaching in U.S. Schools: Results of a National Survey*, Washington, D.C.: Center for Applied Linguistics, 2009.

Ringbom, Håkan, *Cross-Linguistic Similarity in Foreign Language Learning,* Clevedon, UK: Multilingual Matters, 2007.

Rivers, W. P., "Self-Directed Language Learning and Third Language Learners," paper presented at the 30th Annual Meeting of American Council on the Teaching of Foreign Languages, Philadelphia, Penn., November 22–24, 1996.

Rivers, W. P., and E. M. Golonka, "Third Language Acquisition Theory and Practice," in M. Long and C. Doughty, eds., *The Handbook of Language Teaching,* New York: Wiley-Blackwell, 2009.

Robinson, John P., William P. Rivers, and Richard D. Brecht, "Speaking Foreign Languages in the United States: Correlates, Trends, and Possible Consequences," *Modern Language Journal,* Vol. 90, No. 4, 2006, pp. 457–472.

San Francisco State University, Future Students, web page, undated. As of February 3, 2012:
http://www.sfsu.edu/prospect

———, SF State Chinese Language Flagship Partner Program, web page, 2011. As of February 3, 2012:
http://www.cel.sfsu.edu/summerchinese

Schumann, J. H., "Affective Factors and the Problem of Age in Second Language Acquisition," *Language Learning*, Vol. 25, 1975, pp. 209–235.

———, "The Acculturation Model for Second Language Acquisition," in R. C. Gingras, ed., *Second Language Acquisition and Foreign Language Learning,* Washington, D.C.: Center for Applied Linguistics, 1978.

Shachter, J., "Maturational and Universal Grammar," in W. C. Ritchie and T. K. Bhatia, eds., *Handbook of Second Language Acquisition*, San Diego, Calif.: Academic Press, 1996, pp. 159–193.

Shin, H. B., and R. Bruno, "Language Use and English-Speaking Ability: 2000," Washington, D.C.: U.S. Census Bureau Brief, C2KBR-29, October 2003. As of April 5, 2011:
http://www.census.gov/prod/2003pubs/c2kbr-29.pdf

Simon, P., *The Tongue-Tied American: Confronting the Foreign Language Crisis*, New York: The Crossroad Publishing Company, 1980.

Skehan, P., *Individual Differences in Second Language Learning*, London: Edward Arnold, 1989.

Snyder, T. D., and S. A. Dillow, *Digest of Education Statistics 2009*, Washington, D.C.: National Center for Education Statistics, Institute of Education Sciences, U.S. Department of Education, NCES 2010-013, 2010.

Sparks, R. L., "If You Don't Know Where You're Going, You'll Wind Up Somewhere Else: The Case of Foreign Language Learning Disability," *Foreign Language Annals,* Vol. 42, No. 1, 2009, pp. 7–26.

University of California, Los Angeles, Undergraduate Admissions, web page, 2012. As of February 3, 2012:
http://www.admissions.ucla.edu

———, Russian Flagship Center, web page, 2012. As of February 3, 2012:
http://www.russianflagship.ucla.edu

University of Hawaii, Mānoa, Admissions, web page, 2010. As of February 3, 2012:
http://www.manoa.hawaii.edu/admissions

———, Korean Language Flagship Center, 2009. As of February 6, 2012:
http://koreanflagship.manoa.hawaii.edu/

University of Maryland, College Park, Arabic Flagship Program, web page, undated. As of February 3, 2012:
http://www.languages.umd.edu/arabic/flagship/index.html

———, Persian Flagship Program, web page, undated. As of February 3, 2012:
http://www.languages.umd.edu/persian/flagship/index.html

———, Undergraduate Admissions, web page, 2011. As of February 3, 2012:
http://www.admissions.umd.edu/admissions

University of Michigan, Ann Arbor, Arabic Language Instruction Flagship, web page, 2008. As of February 3, 2012:
http://arabicflagship.msu.edu/

———, Undergraduate Admissions, web page, undated. As of February 3, 2012:
http://www.admissions.umich.edu

University of Mississippi, Chinese Language Flagship Program, web page, 2009. As of February 3, 2012:
http://www.olemiss.edu/chinese

———, Office of Admissions & Enrollment Services, web page, 2009. As of February 3, 2012:
http://www.olemiss.edu/admissions

University of Oklahoma, Admissions, web page, 2011. As of February 3, 2012:
http://www.ou.edu/admissions/home.html

———, Arabic Language Flagship Partner Program, web page, 2012. As of February 3, 2012:
http://www.ou.edu/flagship

University of Oregon, Chinese Flagship Program, web page, 2012. As of February 3, 2012:
http://casls.uoregon.edu/uoflagship/en/index.php

———, Office of Admissions, web page, undated. As of February 3, 2012:
http://admissions.uoregon.edu/

University of Rhode Island, Admission, web page, 2011. As of February 3, 2012:
http://www.uri.edu/admission

————, The URI Chinese Language Flagship Partner Program, web page, 2011. As of February 3, 2012:
http://www.uri.edu/chineseflagship/index.html

University of Texas at Austin, Office of Admissions, web page, 2011. As of February 3, 2012:
http://www.utexas.edu/student/admissions

————, Arabic Flagship Program, web page, 2011. As of February 3, 2012:
http://www.utarabicflagship.org

————, Hindi Urdu Flagship, web page, 2012. As of February 3, 2012:
http://www.hindiurduflagship.org

University of Washington, "Transfer Credit Policies," last modified May 5, 2008. As of April 5, 2011:
http://admit.washington.edu/Requirements/Transfer/Plan/CreditPolicies

University of Wisconsin–Madison, Language Institute, Russian Flagship Center, web page, 2010. As of
February 3, 2012:
http://www.languageinstitute.wisc.edu/russian_flagship/index.htm

U.S. Air Force, Air Force Culture, Region & Language Flight Plan, May 2009, pp. 1–21.

U.S. Code, Title 20, Chapter 33, Subchapter 1, Section 1401.

U.S. Department of Defense, Defense Language Transformation Roadmap, Washington, D.C., January 2005.
As of February 16, 2012:
http://www.defense.gov/news/Mar2005/d20050330roadmap.pdf

————, Irregular Warfare (IW), Joint Operating Concept (JOC), Version 1.0, September 11, 2007a.
http://www.au.af.mil/au/awc/awcgate/irregular/iw_joc2_0.pdf

————, Regional and Cultural Capabilities: The Way Ahead, Washington, D.C., October 2007b. As of
February 16, 2012:
http//www.hsdl.org/?view&did=11267

————, National Defense Strategy, Washington, D.C., June 2008. As of February 16, 2012:
http://www.defense.gov/news/2008%20national%20defense%20strategy.pdf

————, Quadrennial Defense Review, Washington, D.C., February 2010. As of February 16, 2012:
http://www.defense.gov/qdr/qdr%20as%20of%2029jan10%201600.PDF

U.S. Department of Education, National Center for Education Statistics, The Condition of Education 2005,
Washington, D.C.: U.S. Government Printing Office, NCES 2005-094, 2005.

U.S. Government Accountability Office, Military Training: DoD Needs a Strategic Plan and Better Inventory
and Requirements Data to Guide Development of Language Skills and Regional Proficiency, Report to
Congressional Committees, Washington, D.C., GAO-09-568, June 2009.

U.S. House of Representatives, House Armed Services Committee, Building Language Skills and Cultural
Competencies in the Military: DoD's Challenge in Today's Educational Environment, Subcommittee on Oversight
and Investigations, November 2008.

Valdes, G., "The Teaching of Heritage Languages: An Introduction for Slavic-Teaching Professionals," in Olga
Kagan and Benjamin Rifkin, eds., The Learning and Teaching of Slavic Languages and Cultures, Bloomington,
Ind.: Slavica, 2000, pp. 375–403.

Weltens, Bert, "The Attrition of Foreign-Language Skills: A Literature Review," Applied Linguistics, Vol. 8,
Spring 1987, pp. 22–38.

Western Kentucky University, Admissions, web page, 2011. As of February 3, 2012:
http://www.wku.edu/Info/Admissions/newhome.html

————, Chinese Flagship Program, web page, 2012. As of February 3, 2012:
http://www.wku.edu/chineseflagship

Yamnill, Siriporn, and Gary N. McLean, "Theories Supporting Transfer of Training," Human Resource
Development Quarterly, Vol. 12, No. 2, Summer 2001, pp. 195–208.